OTHER WORK BY JOSEPH DONAHUE

BOOKS

Before Creation
World Well Broken
Incidental Eclipse
Terra Lucida
Dissolves
Red Flash on a Black Field
Dark Church
The Disappearance of Fate
Wind Maps I-VII
Infinite Criteria
Música Callada
Near Star

CHAPBOOKS

Monitions of the Approach
Terra Lucida
Terra Lucida XV-XX
In This Paradise
The Copper Scroll

TRANSLATION

Zhang Er, *First Mountain* (translated with author)

DISFLUENCY

collected uncollected poems
(1973 - 2023)

JOSEPH
DONAHUE

DOS MADRES

2024

DOS MADRES PRESS INC.
P.O. Box 294, Loveland, Ohio 45140
www.dosmadres.com   editor@dosmadres.com

Dos Madres is dedicated to the belief that the small press is essential to the vitality of contemporary literature as a carrier of the new voice, as well as the older, sometimes forgotten voices of the past. And in an ever more virtual world, to the creation of fine books pleasing to the eye and hand.

Dos Madres is named in honor of Vera Murphy and Libbie Hughes, the "Dos Madres" whose contributions have made this press possible.

Dos Madres Press, Inc. is an Ohio Not For Profit Corporation and a 501 (c) (3) qualified public charity. Contributions are tax deductible.

Executive Editor: Robert J. Murphy

Illustration & Book Design: Elizabeth H. Murphy
www.illusionstudios.net

Cover photograph © Anthony M. Sampas

Typeset in Adobe Garamond Pro & CG Omega
ISBN 978-1-962847-12-4
Library of Congress Control Number: 2024941822

First Edition

ACKNOWLEDGEMENTS

Some of these poems first appeared in *Alea, Columbia, Golden Hand-cuffs Review, Hambone, New Directions in Poetry and Prose, Scrips*i, and *Social Texts*.

COVER PHOTOGRAPH

In Memoriam: Frederick Hunking Horne Jr. (1954-2014)
and Tina Lindegren Horne (1952-2015)

Image captured by Tony Sampas January 7, 2014 during construction of the Richard P. Howe Memorial Bridge, Lowell, Massachusetts at 5:43 pm using a handheld 2010 Nikon D7000 DSLR camera fitted with a workbench converted 1967 Nikkor-P Auto 1:2.5 f=105mm lens.

for Tony Sampas

. . . and light is never so beautiful as in the presence of darkness.

Henry Vaughan

TABLE OF CONTENTS

HEROIC DOLDRUMS

SHADOWS IN THE WATER

CHAOTIC PENDULUM

UNDER THE PRESSURE OF RECENT DEVELOPMENTS

VITA NUOVA

PASSING CLARITIES

KEROUAC SAW THE CROSS

CASUALLY IN FAILING LIGHT

Store window
Mirrored
fire

Far hills
Clouds

A seared

reddish-
orange

looping

motion of
mottle,

over the city.
Hypnotic

drop
above the

river,
the

Hudson
        River

GLANCE BACK

Red mill:
    bricks
  dispel

    into river, into

the river,
the Merrimack

River

   *

Riches   poled
in barges. Canals,
smokestacks,
steeples,
clouds in
black chunks –

   *

River bend
a sunlit flood
A girl gathering
blueberries
in a graveyard
will be your
mother

*

You, as of
yet
      a particle
blowing between
planets,

      *

tending
earthward,

      *

nonetheless,

                  you see
what happens
here, along

the trembling
            Merrimack

      *

See an ambulance
at a curb, a stretcher

floating
across a lawn, see

ancestral
death

*

See children
– your elders –
playing

*

The gregarious one
who will get rich

The mercurial
one who will be
a priest

*

A girl, your
godmother,
has just fallen
from a tree,
breaking her arm

*

What they see,
you see

*

Hoof-clop,
flung slush

– a milkman at twilight
in a snowstorm

*

Holiday
glitter

*

And, at the homes of
those dead in
the war –

*

A gold
star shrouded in

tinsel

KEROUAC SAW THE CROSS

In the Pacific
   night sky: Kerouac
          saw the cross

    *

flaming icon mirroring that dark annihilation
    atop the stone-peaked
         peasant grotto &

    *

   playground
    Golgotha
     – locally

    *

   miraculous –
    above the gloomy
        Merrimack

    *

—but bodiless, now,
      over black rocks,
            ghostly froth

MUSIC LESSON

Orphic lima
beans, pressed

against the
inner ring

by
a damp
coil of inkblot

– glass after glass
line the classroom sill –

        beyond
             which:

     *

a haphazard pro-
cession, into church, of
the devastated,
the family
and friends.

     *

        (And then the

exuberant
classmates, glad
     for the day off –)

   *

Drop down, dove;

     a high school football game:

a beer bottle flung
upwards above the

crowd falls and
strikes

     a boy dead.

   *

Through the
back window

my mother the music teacher
can see the steps of

the church, surge
of mourners into
the service   all while

in front of her, thirty-

odd upturned Catholic
grammar school faces

get ready to sing.

      *

              (After the funeral, as the cars
              heading for the cemetery
              pull into a single line,

              boys are hauling
              wreathes of

              lavender and
              pearl-colored flowers
                        through a light rain.)

MUSIC LESSON   II

The future dead might stop
me in a store,

at a party,
saying, of

some long ago
hit, this

is, will be,
the song.

*

Saying promise me
you will sing

this song
I love,

when it's
my day?

*

(Today the dead
boy's friend sings.)

*

After a funeral
a card might say:

While you sang

that song
we felt

our loved one
right there,

as if alive again

standing

beside us.

DREAM, 1973

Path of shadow along
a long stone wall.

The black of
my cassock
is turning red . . .

Elders pass
and nod.

In the shade,
on a stone bench
my mother just
happens to be
sitting,

eyes some color
other than would be

seen in

waking life.

"We're all
so proud that
you're now
a bishop . . ."

*

"I need to leave
the church.
Mom," I say.

"To serve

God
is

to kill
yourself."

DREAM PAINTINGS

ANTEROOM SHIVERS

But I knew I was haunted and said nothing.

Kerouac

Spun from the metals of
the Second World War,
an amusement park.
I brush spiritual
dust from an
old nickelodeon.

*

Revolutionary pamphlets
turn to red-throated birds
atop the drugstore.

A high-pitched shearing.

Song, or pages torn off
in the street wind?

Then, loosed from
the army convoy cages,
glue horses clomping
on the highway.

Or drifting, hesitant,
across a parking lot.

*

Conduit hum through the building.
Fraying metal at a dockside.
A red girl billowing
in a stairwell.

*

First, find a raccoon
dead in a desert. Taste it.
Taste it before the
vultures come down
from the rocks.

*

The current carries
chestnut husks,
green and spiky,
turning in slow circles
across the sidewalk before
sailing for the islands
down a black river
through what seems to be
laundromat foam.
The street achieves
a delicacy a breath
would disturb.

*

What is that book about?
Behavioral Deviance.

A woman with a crayon is striking out
certain characters from novels.

A yellow light revolves.
My fever sways out, touching
a pillowcase of rain.

Tires piled in yellow pits.

Houses lost behind trees.

A can, rimmed with red paint.

Sink, sky, into dark clouds.

*

(But the clouds are stolen highway signs
used by hunters
to cross soggy spots.)

On the table, a coyote's jawbone
juts from a red box.

*

My mother bickers with moving men
about the cost of carrying

a coffin back
into the house while

I notify the hospital.

*

A line survives a dream:
The heuristic face of
a priest in moonlight.

*

Waking, then, distressed
by doctrines of
pure mind.

*

The first
fish entering the
dye spill feels lightheaded.

Everyone in the church
for predawn Mass
is frightened.

Pilate, with his men
in the back, in the dark.

Is the one they hunt
hiding here?

*

The cement seems weathered,
like tobacco smoke was sucked through it
for twenty years.

As if somewhere inside each
slab a whiteness
left from the light

strikes deep as the sand
concedes to concrete.

A last beam of sunlight
resting in the crevices,
reveals a blind spot,

a cool square of earth
between an old stump
and a car fender.

A boy begins to kick
the dirt away,
and the stones.

*

Bare woods around the playing field

where the half time band
marches in the shape

of a television.

*

Half-buried bathtub.

Sky-blue enamel.

Mary, flaking into wind.

*

And here, an entire
building of anterooms,

a psychiatric wing

where a patient
waits to be called.

DREAM PAINTING

Yellow

peppering

the red filling

the window

on the far wall,

like a field of

goldenrod

flickering up

around the red of

a sad face.

BOMB SHELTER

The streets glistened
red and blue, fresh
in the after-rain.
You said let's find
somewhere to lie down.
It turned out, this was Boston,
near your dorm room
where we were first
lost in delight.
We find our way to
an abandoned
bomb shelter,
bedding spread
on the grimy floor.
Derelicts homesteading
there are happy to
see us together
again. They offer us
the shadows.

SIX SONGS FOR CHILDREN

the mistaken child

That first year

   of "fallout"

      past the apple tree

       fallout falling

         white blossoms.

     muddy fields
     under

       summer snow

and a boy in the fading
   dark, walking

   barefoot over

      the drifts.

summer house

A house
"on the water,"
      on stilts,
a brick house.
    A rope ladder
dropping down
from a hole
in the floor of
      the kitchen.
At midnight,
the tide rises,
     the house floats.

theft

Taped shut
in a tin box and

tamped into the earth,
          the pearl earrings,

& the boy hoping
the box
would dissolve
in a stream flowing
forever beneath his feet

& two minnows
burst the tin,

the tiny, shiny
          fish fluttering
                    far upstream

brushing the hand
of a girl drawing water

to be
pearls again,
be set gleaming
half hidden
sunlit,

be, again,
earrings,

amid

tucks of

her freshly
brushed hair.

returning

The prodigal does not feel
all that penitent.
He thinks forgiveness
a trick with words.

A parapet and broken wall
molded from ice
fill the yard of his old house.
The children who live here now

are in for dinner.
His father does not hammer
the frozen latch and let him in
as he might have in life.

The evening wind would creak the gate,
but the gate is gone.
The snow fort rises
cold as a household,

but he feels no loss.
He follows God's advice,
which is indistinguishable
from silence.

vigil

Grace was taken from the earth.
Hospitals rose up.
The priest on call hardly
ever sleeps much.
All hours the ill
turn penitent.
Some wonder aloud
why the light with
which God heals
them breaks
their bodies down.

orphanage

The children hold out their arms
and imitate airplanes.
They outrun August,
they cool in the sunlit rain.
To watch them, you might think
their abandonment
had ended.

A faint steam fills the street,
but you can still find home –
it's where the clouds move to
when they darken.

SIX SONGS FOR ADULTS

Penance

The priest in his confessional hears lives
pass in error. He can only counsel
and absolve. He is only the instrument
of absolution. He can only pass in error
through the bleak lives of his parishioners
like a black wind down an idle street
or a breath through a broken instrument.
The priest in his confessional derives
the one sin which underlies the many.
He can only pass in terror judgment
upon the parishioner in the dark
who wants to be absolved of the life
he claims is an empty, idle street
where he finds in his hands a broken instrument,
where he wanders like a sick, black wind.
The priest in his confessional hears lives
pass in terror, which only his counsel
can absolve. The parishioner derives
a judgement from the bleak life of the priest
who has longed at times for death in the dark,
a black wind at the end of an idle street
who finds in his hands a broken instrument.

Marriage

Of blessedness, what remnant. A chalice
lofted in the celebrant's hand, recollected in hell.
The bride and the bridegroom are joined.
The sun above them on this blue afternoon
is a lofted chalice. For each of them
hell is recollection. For each of them
hell and blessedness are joined. Blue afternoon.
The father of the bride will not live long.
Already he is a remnant of what he was,
a chalice filled with recollection, lofted on
a blue afternoon. Of blessedness what remnant.
The bride and the bridegroom, the Eucharist
taken from the celebrant's hand, the blue
afternoon joined with a recollection of hell
where the ghost of the bride joins her father,
where a hand has set them in a sulphur chalice
hotter than the sun on a blue afternoon.
The desire of the bride will not live long,
a chalice she will drink dry. The bridegroom's hand
will place her in hell. For each of them hell
is the ghost of desire, the bread and wine
a remnant of what once was. The sun above them
lofted by an unseen celebrant, a blessedness
where hell was once believed to be.
The father of the bride will not live long.
Long enough to see his daughter's unhappiness,
long enough to pray the bridegroom burn in a hell
at the heart of the sun. On a blue afternoon
a chalice lofted in the celebrant's hand
sanctifies a marriage that will not live long.
Long enough for a child, a remnant who will
drink dry the chalice and cast it down,

cast down the Eucharist from the celebrant's hand.
Who will live long enough to see the gold robes
of the celebrant, the ghost of his grandfather,
as the bride and the bridegroom are joined,
are photographed, on a blue afternoon on
a church lawn, the chalice of the sun lofted
by an unseen blessedness, bright and distant
as hellfire to the saved.

Last Rites

The priest anoints each extremity with oil,
removes the relic from the hands of the dead.
The night no darker than a hospital room,
than a relic that should have been a miracle.
Those who love the dead loiter in a corridor,
a corridor brighter than a soul entering the world.
The priest anoints the night that takes
the dead from his hands.

The son removes the relic from the hands
of the dead. Night no darker than a corridor
that leads the soul to hell. Those who love the dead
walk down a corridor that ends in hell.
The priest unfolds his purple stole in a hospital
room at night. The priest anoints a man
deserted by the Holy Spirit. The hospital stands
amid factories. The souls rise up like dirty smoke.
The son feels the father has anointed him with his death.

Night removes the dead from the hands of the living,
thinks the nurse in the hospital corridor.

Hospitals are factories that turn the living to smoke,
thinks a man called from his bed to watch
his brother die. The damned are condemned
to build temples out of dust, thinks the priest
who absolves the soul of a man who cannot hear him.
The soul is what anoints the living. When the soul
vanishes, what remains? Oil at the extremities,
thinks the son watching the priest.

Take this night from my hands, thinks each
called in turn to the hospital. The damned could suffer
no worse than to walk down this corridor a last time,
thinks the wife who asks the priest about the Spirit.
The night no darker than a blackened temple,
the deathbed an altar each kneels before. A cross
etched in oil anoints the eyes of the dead. In the room:
brother, wife and son. Night has taken
brother, husband, and father from their hands,
left for each a cup.

The priest anoints each extremity with oil.
The Word of the Father is a temple I have beaten
into dust, thinks each for whom the corridor
of night ends in a deathbed. While I slept
my brother died, thinks the man who sips
from a paper cup outside a hospital room.
The priest puts away his purple stole,
looks out the windows at the factories.
Smoke rises. Rises from a hospital in hell.
The wife removes the ring from the hand of the dead.
I am the relic of what he was, thinks the son.
No one expects the Holy Spirit to return
to an altar no more than a deathbed. No one
removes the relic from the hands of the dead.
None drink willingly the cup they are given.

Baptism

A brilliant water dumped on the dead ground,
that's what life is without heaven or hell to end it
thinks the mother who is praying for her son.
The father checks the new camera, worries the light
on this fogged October day is insufficient.
The fogged day a golden font which absolves
unhappiness between man and wife.

With a cruet of brilliant water the priest
rinses the offense from the brow of the son,
unlaces the child's white gown and anoints
his back with the cross he is asked to bear.
The mother recites the baptismal prayers,
The father prays that his son will please him.
The child, cradled over the golden font

is a Host held aloft by blessed fingers
above the cup of sacrifice. With oil the priest
makes a cross on the newborn's back, though
he knows most crucifixions take place in the heart,
the heart a staggering hill where a god is put to death.
No fogged limbo now, there is a heaven to end it,
thinks the mother for whom the son redeems

the unhappiness between man and wife.
The overcast October feels grey as a cathedral
on the stone steps of which she will stand
photographed by her husband in his dark blue suit,
the day a golden font cupping brilliant tears.
Or so the son will think, deep in the life to come.
The priest daubs the newborn's tongue with salt,

salt mopped from the brow of Adam
who recalls his offense, who drinks his cup
deep in the hell of the life to come.

Eucharist

And must there be
a Judas at each Mass
maybe by the pillar,
maybe in a line of
communicants,
long cold stone
aisle floor, begging
for bread? Is no table
properly attended
without a betrayer?

Adam, in Hell

Mountain & abyss.
Cresting sun.

Sky: sheet metal
pulled from a furnace.

The jammed plow
divvies up a root.

Hell's unharrowed.
Adam burns, opening

the ground for a sowing,
a blight of fire.

Generations are passing.
Their lament and rage

fill the wind
but the wind does not reach him.

No cross here
but Adam's shadow.

No crow or locust,
the valley winds into smoke.

Gnarled in rock,
taking root in flame –

no seeds but
images.

NO MANSION

WHERE AFFECTION HOLDS
NO STEADY MANSION   I

That was me, then,

      the new part-time

            amanuensis to

a notable
    nationally syndicated

tabloid
    astrologer,

a seeress
who foresaw

      the death of JFK,

        who, now, every day,

on behalf of callers
to her rented

phone lines, offers,

        pre-taped

weeks   in advance,

insights for every

sign. She,

Jeanne Dixon,

intuits
the confusion of

    the heavens.

    *

I had lucked out, got this job at
    the precise moment of my own

      unprecedented

        amorous
          catastrophe –

a fantastic new love,
    a grad student
        like myself,

both of us derelicts of

literature,

both   stridently

impractical

she, an inebriate of
        The Wings of the Dove

me,
        besotted
by Sydney's

Arcadia . . .

                *

Newsstands padlocked.
                Papers strung in bundles.

Rooftops
brightening, sky the

the silvery base of a candlestick

still glowing
            beneath
                    millennia of tarnish.

Exceedingly late.
Going home euphoric.

        (Tomorrow night
                    is tonight!

                Will she wear
                        that purple sash?)

*

prophecy

In the 18th century
        Jonathan Swift amused
                        himself, each year,
    rereading,
            on his birthday,

the Book of Job.

In modernity,
            a Celt given to
                    melancholy and melodrama
            might open,
    by way of contrast,

on his twenty-fifth natal day,

        the Book of
                Lamentations:

"Our inheritance
        is turned to strangers,
                our houses to aliens."

*

(But on my birth certificate
        an alchemical sun stamped
                        on a page of the sky!)

                *

Was this my celestial admission?

Just by adding, to the text mailed from afar

by the famed and alcoholic

astrologer, often

                ill-disposed,

the script to be taped by
the voice actress,

(a former Miss Rheingold)

        "Chances are"
            "This could be."

My divine charge, above all:

Call forth any provocative

        intimations.

                Add more love!

Help depressed Jeanne foresee.

"Get ready! The night
                looks great
                        for romance!"

                *

            prophecy

How Love and I lay awake
            and planned a pilgrimage.

Country house,
her ancestral estate, no,
                        her villa, she said.

The fountains would be
cascading for my arrival.
A bed turned down, for me,
and, when the sun flooded the pond,
we would meet on the
                        porticoes for
                    pastries freshly made
                        by the kitchen staff.

I imagined her robe,
the one she'd have there,
– even more stunning
            than what she wore now.
The driver will be waiting,
she said, Friday, after work.
"He is a white Russian,
dependable,
though prone to
            religious fanaticism.

He assisted my family
in their escape to Brooklyn, long ago.
I will be waiting there for you
by the harpsichord,
ready for the evening recital.

Later, we'll steal off into the woods,
uncertain and excited, with
        so many secrets
           to tell each other."

      *

In such deep heat,
the most erotic
        thought
           is simply this:
that she sleeps with
     a glass of ice water
               by her bed.
On a night apart from her,
I can't sleep from
wondering if
    the shifts of
        melting ice wake her,
and what, assuming she is alone,
she thinks of, curving
upward, on her elbow,
into the humidity,
for a cool sip?

      *

(Below her apartment window: boxes of
apples, plums, mangoes

                    fruit-stand gifts, to or from
                                    the gathering dawn.)

          *

          St. Luke's

Emergency in green lights
              – brilliant, for blocks.

By the triage vending machine, a placard:

*Patients have the right to deny treatment once the
consequences of such a denial have been determined.*

Below it, of further pertinence:

*Death expenses for victims of violent crime will be
paid by the Federal Government.*

The most unstable of
of my philandering
roommate's three loves
in the depths of abandonment
          had not,
          as she apparently intended,
done herself in. The gash
needed no stitches.

There was, clearly,
when I came home and
was the one, in lieu of her love,
to find her, by the smashed lamp,
with blood encrusted wrists,
sipping wine,
time enough
    to get her coat.

     *

The next weekend,
       I'm distracted, escorting the daughter
          of a family friend
        to a Port Jefferson wedding.
Beautiful bride,
         cream-colored gown.

A rambunctious retriever
chased stones flung
           into the muck.
Spattered and obedient,
the dog brought back
the stone
        and set it at my feet.

     *

    High ceilings, Persian carpets, open bar.

A jeu d'esprit at The Yale Club . . .

Senseless largesse:
Free tickets from the boss,

a pre-release screening,

Polanski's *Tess* –

> Of all love's
> secret loves, so
> vulnerable, in the dark,
>> Nastassja Kinski!)

*

Sometimes I'd be on loan,
    one boss to another,
        taking inventory

                    for a firm that put up
illuminated rooftop taxicab ads
all over New York.

A warehouse like
    those on crime shows
        where the police seize
the stolen jewels,
    find the finely parsed heroin
        wrapped tight as silverware
            in a linen napkin.

I'm bored, but on the lookout,
    amid dusty bolsters
        of drab fabric,

for something valuable,
                something I could take

                and never be caught.
Not a trinket, a perception.

A turn of thought,
                found right there,

amid crates of fluorescent light bulbs
and the brightly colored
Marlboro paste-ups,

perhaps even, despite
the dreary depths of the day,
a passing clarity, a true poetic image!

                *

                prophecy

"I'm an only child," she, suddenly sad,
        "And both my parents
                fell out with their families . . . "

                *

                dream

                Acrid white clouds
                feathered the air around

the three figures,
made it hard to tell

who the two were, so
fiercely arguing, together

on the foremost seat
of the boat, while

the figure behind
the couple, the

dreamer within the
dream, lifted the oars,

looked down, lost
in water clear

and calm as a lake
high in the mountains,

though this was
a flooded field.

Beneath the grey
glaze of the water

could be seen,
if only by

the dreamer,
farmhouses,

drifting by, trees,
reaching upwards.

*

At the end of
the street,
        a cathedral,

emphatically unfinished,
        Saint John the Divine,

lacking a chapel,

the tabernacle

      stuffed with porn.

*

Our elation

felt indestructible,

thereby confirming,

we were, would be,

immortal.

        (But then there's
        that pain, of
        which
        Immortals
        are said to be
        unaware.)

*

As a child, her thick black hair, her
intense, self-vacating gaze.

Between her labor lawyer mother,
in business dress, and her father,
the renowned designer
        and secret sculptor,
                in his bow tie.

Passport picture:

American Marxists
of the 1930s,
and their beguiling
daughter, off to Russia,
        once their motherland.

*

    "When a game needed tears
I hummed Russian tunes," she said.

*

Travelling, now, if only on a getaway weekend
        we huddled in a train station.

*

Our caution
simply readied us

      for extravagance.

In her case, this might mean:

purple jeans, a purple
jersey, and red nail polish.

    *

Absorbed, even
as we were, in an article
about a fashion model brutalized
        by a parking lot attendant.

    *

Sensing ourselves saved.

    *

      Drifting off, later,
        on her parents' bed.

Waking, she woke me,
a nervous joke about having
wildly reenacted the "primal scene."
Then a marvelous meal of
      eggplant, mushrooms,
              onions, red peppers,
                        rice, and

her self-proclaimed wizardry, the spice.

     *

Later vexations
      in night's
         shadows:

         the slippery fish of
                a diaphragm.

     Still later: "God damn it!
       We forgot about
         the swimming pool!"

A sheet round her nakedness,
she rushes down the stairs, into
the too-quiet yard.

     (*prophecy*

A pump turned on
   nine hours ago will raise
         the water line.)

Still later: she breaks out
        a book on Jungian typology
                pinpointing herself:

"Introverted intuitive!

            I notice things but
        I associate
            so fast I forget
                where I started.
I'll see that wine bottle
        and, the next minute,
                    knock it over."

        *

Out in the evening
the water in the pool and
the water on the concrete around the pool
a single mirror filled with
            houselights,
        immense trees, and the night.
The pump gone silent; the spout, underwater.

A leaf or two, drifting.

Down the
embankment, the
            overflow
                shining in the garden.

        *

prophecy

The streets will lack all élan.
                  I will wonder if she's awake
at her window, three blocks up, where
      barge lights can be seen
            moving toward the ocean
   Melville said   "permits no records."

*

sunset

Clouds, radiant, as who would not be,
freed by nightfall from looking at the earth.

WHERE AFFECTION HOLDS
NO STEADY MANSION II

There went the epoch
of delight between the two,
blowing with trash on the street.

*

That the stars oversaw
such despondency seemed
        not quite
                credible.

*

At times,
walking home
from an Italian movie
        or discussing what
was missing from
        the life of this
                or that third person
their true dispute
        found them,
and their humiliation
frightened them.

*

Shining, far beyond them,
   Blake's gates of paradise.
     Mutual forgiveness of every vice . . .

   *

What wisdom
could these two
   ever accept,
   caught, as they
were, in the
neediest of
speculations?

   *

The quiet
gliding of the
   canoe
     gives the
illusion of peace.
Gives the illusion
   the two
     there, on the water,
       are peaceful.

   *

Fireflies animate the rain which itself
enlivens the green abundance.

The piano drills she
chances upon and plays

cannot quicken
the moment's

severity.

    *

How
many more
      afternoons

could they outdo
the Creator's cloud-born
  turbulence?

True, neither could
merely, by thinking of it,

bend trees,
      or drive leaves
           into the empty pool.

But each *can*
blacken the sky,

and,
     with a word,
turn

      abundance
         to dust.

*

Now and then
the future unfurled its bright banner.
They saw what a rag it was.

*

Inconclusive
night. Each would,
were it possible, blame
the other. But who
can find fault
in a situation so
"complex?"

*

Bells ring Bach.
        The sun falling.

*

Despondency and Panic
        descending like angels.

*

Day,
a dark pit.
Neither making much
effort to crawl out.

     *

In these depths,
    she feels alone,
only her cry for companion.

     *

Leaves shining
on the trees
     tended to
    reminded them
       of bareness.

     *

(What was so dispiriting
was less the expulsion,
each independently concluded,
    but just to be called
      before the Creator –

in the garden
at the close of day,

that first
      insight.)

    *

To call the Merlot
      they sipped
         "Spiritual Death"

      would be overly
         consoling.

    *

The wind from the river brought voices
that said all is about to be

demonstrably

hopeless.

    *

It was the image of
sunlight through a window
that most troubled them.

A life recollected as light, but was,
in point of fact, darkness.

*

It was the idea that
light could glorify
all they owned (right
down to a shirt so torn
only a saint would wear it
and with which one
or the other wiped
the dust from a table)
and leave them
unchanged.

*

Apropos of all this
a friend said:
A glimpse of
the promised land
doesn't much interest
either of you, does it?
For you two, only
affliction in
the wilderness
will do.

*

They sat out
in a sun-shower
and watched the pool,

the drops
too slight to
ripple the calm.

What last
grace was this,

that they could see
the rain's shadow
on the pool's

        white floor?

   *

They spent the evening
sponging grime
from a discarded office fan.

The intent with
which they scoured
each blade was the last

of what
united them.

SONG OF SONGS

Last night the
     coastal mansions
         on the cliffs glowed,
as did the fog around them.

     *

Between wave-breaks
       wings can be heard.
In a barrel, a gull frees
a cheese cracker,
rips it, flutters,
     scatters trash.

     *

The stalk quivers,
     then the petal. The
         only breeze

the lingering of

a drunk
hornet.

     *

*My right
arm around your
waist, I was a king
held captive in
your hair.*

THE SCHEMES OF SLEEP

Pale cluster: shoots
  at stream's edge,
    Paradisal waters

that Dante drank.

Her eye, tint of
  first foliage and
    the dress she danced in –

the gallery lit for a party.

The photographer compares the past to a print.
  The present decides
    what colors I give it.

Forms appear in
  multicolored fire,
    that realm of her touch.

Burnished arc of copper
  and fragrant shops . . .
    I am a slave

crossing the desert.

The gold I have stolen
                will make me a god.

Brush of hand,
                knee to nape.

Deer tremble in a mist.

All's adrift.

        Mind and desire,
each breathing life into the other.

Renovations
        and coffee scent.

"You won't believe who I was with last night!"

En route to new love through
        a street fair's extravagance.
                The kind of sleep

you get beside
        someone

                whose face you
                        prefer to all dreams.

KIN AND CONCENTRATION

A NOTEBOOK OPEN IN IRELAND

Wet stones, bright shade, fading tremble, day-old detonations, stepping off the ferry, 1974, buying a notebook, cheap, school assignment pages, to be my *Book of Kells*. I would embellish sacred script. I would hosannah starving martyrs. I would write long love letters to Bernadette Devlin.

DREAM

Leaning down, a doctor says: "Don't breathe."

Beside him, huge, fresh from the death squad,

the squad that just shot you,

(Rocks. Pits. Wreckage. Bright sky. A field.
The crime, a sudden flame in your hand.)

a black man. He, too, wants, now,

for you to live. He's famous.
He' s Rosie Grier.

He knelt beside

the dying Robert Kennedy,

in the pantry of the Ambassador hotel . . .

*

By train, by car, by carriage, by foot, deep into the woods,
into the north and incognito, I'm travelling.

An inn appears, lit up but gloomy.
Fellow escapees opt to stay the night,
though it's clear: I should flee.

Witty, cruel, welcoming, the proprietor
is more like a sheriff or a sergeant.

He's like Robert Duval
in *The Great Santini*, and very loud.

*

Not knowing who I am, he says
I've wronged him. He's eloquent. Angry.

If anyone has seen the him that is me,
he would love, he says, just love,

to have a word.

*

"At first your disguise worked well," he says.

"But you kept changing it. It's exactly like,

the poem you are revising.

(A priest in a hospital at night

gives last rites to a dying man.)

"The first draft had promise,"

the Great Santini says,

"But you've ruined it."

*

Were circumstances other it would be

great to see them. They are, after all,

notables from my childhood,

the firing squad that shot me dead.

I want to either

A) cry out in hatred,

or B) put on a Walkman and
hide under my bed.

It's getting hard to enjoy the party.

Also, I'm in love with a fellow grad student,

a beautiful young woman who greets me
at the door of a cottage at the edge of the woods.

*

In the waking world she barely knows me,
but in the dream, we were once lovers.

*

At the door, two priests, sent, they say,
to arrest me. The older is gleeful to have caught me.

He climbs the cottage stairs. At the top, a pay phone.
He calls the Vatican while, from below,
the younger argues on my behalf.

The younger priest is a woman.
A large cross hangs from her neck.

In keeping with her incendiary rage,
her close-cropped hair is red.

Then, overheard from the payphone:

Who could ever side against the church?

My advocate shoots back a phrase
that will thrill me for years to come:

One who wants to kill the ineffable!

     *

Past the barbed wire fence in Central Park
ringing my enclosure, my prison,
autumnal hills go golden.

     *

It turns out I can't be re-killed!

My enthusiasm, however,

is less than what it might be.

My lawyer has his secretary

record my new grievance:

Imprisoned with me is a poet.
His name is Dante.

He has no paper, no pencils.
He's got nothing to read.

*

On my way back to my detention compound

I pass through elegant, well-tended neighborhoods.
They don't feel like Manhattan.

They feel like some unknown, distant city
that I'll live in, years from now.

*

A beautiful, pearl-handled switchblade lands
at my feet. The knife is wiped clean,

but it still looks bloodied.

KIN AND CONCENTRATION

however much each of us
chooses our own
kin and
concentration

Charles Olson

Slapdash, that
genealogy. Wind.
Brown paper bag chart,
rippling & nailed to the wall . . .
Topping the pyramid:
an Irishman in a coffin ship.
Death date and one trait: high
cheekbones, these are the certainties.
Other names, inked in, those
known for a bad deed
or odd whim, one or two,
pure virtue. The mentally ill
and the magnanimous
are copied out, are
equals now. The
reflective among the
living note new details
drifting into awareness
through sunlit fog
not to be recalled,
but to be called back,
to take a place amid
more animate facts:
the redhead, blue eyed,
in a blue bathing suit.
the kerchiefed in-law
between jolts of chemo

who lends fragility
to the feast.

*

Heat and light are
are simply the truer
content of their talk.
Smoke washes white,
over water. Hidden rock.
A motorboat founders.
Mild cries for assistance,
offshore, quite close.
Those calling are
not ancestors, though
the mist itself might be:
criminal and priest resolved,
compounded, burned off.
And the one disinherited,
the one silent at the table
the one who hawked
oranges in Boston
the one who closed
the deal in Carolina
are coast-bound, a cloud,
a blank shimmer, shot
through with beams of
white sun beyond which
the fishermen praised
by Olson still sail out
nets down, after dawn
as the sun whitens, amid
the tankers and regattas

lost in noon's glitter.
More rare: what one,
now, calls all to see:
black fin of a nuclear sub
easing back to the naval base.

*

Not long until the living
crowd out the dead.

*

When is the twilight
where they are the kin
of fire and not just charred
sticks the tide takes out,
where each is seen clearly
and yet honored, where
speech heals, words
redeem the oblivion
of all relation; a place
held in mind which
holds the mind.

*

The chart flaps,
tatters, dampens

with night, talk
flares out. Bodies
dates, all etched in.

*

Rain falls in sunlight.

White mist shimmers
above dark water.

Scrub grass rattles in the wind.

Through the fog,

the moon.

WET SHOES

Wasn't ready
for the rain, wind
driving it

incorrect change,
bus driver, door closing
empty curb at night no one

to ask how else
can I get there,
curses, wet shoes . . .

Not that I don't plan
but the plans I make tend to be
pillars of flame leading into a desert

I find myself at the
discretion of scorpions
left to die

no habitat in sight
no angelic dwelling
not even

a well dug pit
to chasten
the remains.

In that first
estrangement
no more readily . . .

WHERE AFFECTION HOLDS
NO STEADY MANSION   III

Cluster. Orange adrift on green.
The possible needed
further proof:

         a path
into jungle: wet leaves
a shining that could
refute all lack.

       *

Your kick,
your sleek black
swimsuit with green
hieroglyphs

some designer
stole from a stone.

         (O Nile,
         O tangled
         branches of
         desire!)

       *

Blue inlet.
Horse nipping the dirt.
My ghosts mix into green

mountain,
aquamarine
rondure.

*

Sky, violet and gold. Etched
cloud a white gown, for idle
hours as the pills wear off.

*

Green ocean, white sand.
Windsurfers billow by while
you count out your dose.

*

You can't go out in the sun.
Too much light is toxic.
You rail, for a moment,
in the cool of
the hotel room,
against psychopharmacology
that would balance

present moment
with present place.
The disrelation
makes you ill.
I was fine
until I really
wanted to be fine.
Then all hell broke loose.

*

Our creed
of disbelief, –

That the bodily
and the exotic
are one.

*

The pulp
and the replenishment.
The blade, and the open fruit.

*

(But we have
always enjoyed
things less

than our ideas
about those things.)

    *

Continents drift, from and toward,
through the vast ripple of the living sea,

that blue table, set against all hunger.

Thought sweeps me into jagged depths.

And if we picked the wrong island
and the hurricanes of the symbolist soul

are tearing up the world elsewhere,

there's still water and wind and repose.
And the labor that lightens the burden of rest.

    *

        (I didn't love you.
        Another's face,
        the gaze of
        a woman
        I hardly knew,
        rose in your place.
        I kept it there.)

    *

Last night
fever shook you
as wind

a green stalk.

Face–
cloth folded
over the ice
bucket's

rubble.

*

Night burns off and
fruit juice brings your quickness

back,

      swimmer,

energetic letter,
green lines breaking the blue.

Diamond light of waterdrops spun from your arms,

O Caribbean
jewel,

your name, you once told me,
means, in Hebrew,

given of God.

II

The chatter of the guide blows off the earth.

Silence, broken by a goat, wild, curled in the grass.

The grey muck, the crater's runoff, a hot stream
that pours down into greenness

as if to say the final moment, that
end of elemental division is
forever going on.

The beginning as well continues, the island's
endpoint still lifting from the sea.

The dream of the hidden architect's hand unfolds.
Sea the blue of the single parrot feather falling
into a lush clutch of thicket.

The Holy Ghost is a jungle bird.

Yellow and white and green, lime green,
the drench of Sulphur, the curl of steam clouds,

the seething that provokes the living earth.

The cluster of cocoa beans, red petals that crest
the treetops and tremble and bend as

a sea breeze stirs mountains and valley.

Chalky crust. Clear surface. Deadly pool green

as foliage, too turbulent to hold an image
save the scalded bones of lamb or goat.

Thick leaves, rocky juts in partial light.

A sun shower strafes the road,
dampens the scalded patch, wets

the crystals split wide and sold, geodes,
their green stare looking up at the sky

on the boat ride back from the hot springs,
held out in the hand of the beautiful
young doctor from Queens.

     *

Scent of abundance, mingling with hell smoke.
Then, the pure wind from the ocean.

     *

*Pastness is only
an abstraction. The actuality,
the body of feeling, is alive and here.*

SOD'S BROOD

Blue & orange
flicker of an ill-tuned newscast
your sick-mate slept in the face of.

You jokes about the
upcoming vacation you
didn't take.

Avoiding one last outrage –
that a Droney die
in England.

*

What
Celtic chalkscrawl
might astound this altitude

or the lowly
regions of red & gold,
what tribute however

vaporous
scratch here,
translated as I am

northward this
peak foliage weekend
flying home, & to your wake.

*

Disputations,
wisecracks. Your
disheveled passion

pushed the broadcast on
a living copy out over the wire
(Noon. You're at the mike

waterglass in hand . . .)
through galaxies
& into utter absence.

If I spin the dial the hour
of night one can pick up distant cities
& wait with excitement for the DJ

to state the origin point of his voice
would physics ever permit me again to hear you
hashing out, say, Vietnam,

with the shut-in
you dubbed
"The Philosopher?"

*

What
marked your Mass:
I saw the Host as tragic, as

Greek, not an
Apollonian sunburst above the cup
but subject to the wine . . .

Heft of coffin, squeal of
rollers built into the tailgate of the
hearse,

flush & emphatic
the corpulent padre
closes the book.

The Jackie Gleason
of the Catholic Church
quipped which pallbearer?

Forgive me, father.
Forgive me Jim, who
was not my father.

Rest beyond ritual
four stones up & over
from my ancestral hill,

amid Keegans,
Reillys, Fitzpatricks
& Gilbrides.

*

But in our other
religion, of speech
& dream,

in our well-
liquored holy writ,
our enthused & rude

blasphemies,
what crux
elucidates you?

Earth's dream?
Birth's grieve.
Sod's brood,

Mr. Finn.

    *

However the facts are
scrambled on the wires
however late the papers are

in their bleak report
however much grief mingles with the feast
the smoking dish Sarah sets on the table

spiced tomato juice
on a sunlit, makeshift bar
however much we divide the rack of

outrageous ties
a vivid man steps amid spirits,
leaves wife and sons and daughters

& the black-suited
& pale associates
of Mahoney

who tip the flowers to hide the pit.
The son-in-law's final bravo was not mine,
though it might have been. We turned

& you were handed over
to an earth not at all the dust Christ mixed
with spittle and rubbed into the beggar's blind eyes

and he saw, or some
other miracle of figural speech.
(But you will live again

for the ones who can
truly invoke you.)

     *

Flying back, I see what you see:
sparkle of New York below.
Single, black cloud.

Shunted, now. A loop
over the coast,
hurricane closing.

Fabulous, the maze of
lamp-lit neighborhoods
below and black, black ocean.

TREE OF MANY

Not the solitary
tree Frost imagined.

Not the light
lost in the limbs.

Not romance & catcall
& brothers racing through

the utmost thrust.
Not the *crow's nest*

its glimpse of the river.
Not the handhold or bole,

the ascent
cousins taught me

in the twilight of 1964,
in autumn's copper whirlwind.

No stories
or lives scored

in the bluish grey bark.
Not any initial known

among
the myriad.

Not my name cut here
& not the suicide locked in a tree

in Dante's hell
uttering nothing but the past.

No blade stroke,
no matter how legible.

Nothing now but the untold.
The core.

The hidden voices.
The warring

& rhapsodic
gods.

THE SWIMMER'S BILLOW

dispels into green.
Seasons dispel into the froth of her kick
her clutch and release of ocean,
into the rippling scar on her neck,
the excised death,
into the pulse of thought as
knees cocked back
asprawl in blue and early light.
He kneels, enters her.
Tangles of belly, breast, bands of hair.
Aspirant grip
in a room above a harbor where
inadvertent
histories mingle.
Branches a thrash of gold.
Wet green tufts streaked with yellow.
this tropical drenching
mid-October.
Hurricane's utterance heard
by two walking now out and into
convolutions
of air and water,
figura of Dante's
confessional rapture.
No night matches this,
this walking out, this first
morning together.
No living water as blue as her blue coat,
silvered lightly, the wind visible
against her living form.
The silence turns fluent.
Grey of sky, water, stone

and froth whirling and exploding,
earth no longer muck
but the tarnished embodiment of light.
Because a woman in a blue coat walks here,
leads a man who has just loved her
to a hidden pool where rises across an inlet
the red outline of
Purgatory Rock.
Flicker and surge.
Hue of hair,
of limbs entwined.
The green jab and
undulation of her glance
past meadow and mansion,
drenched briar, folds of stone,
to a deep tide pool,
hidden and full.

THE DEATH OF KEROUAC

for Tony Sampas

Old wall lamps, tiny chains snap the light on. Soapstone
sink, faucets like outdoor spigots, grooved spouts to hook up
a hose if needed. Dinner served on a marble-topped heirloom
laundry table. On it, a doctor did ear surgery on a black-haired
girl who would become my aunt. Desolate linoleum. Flimsy
metal shelves. Cork bulletin board. Vocab words. Choir dates.
My father has just unfolded *The Lowell Sun.*

*

In the doorway, I'm fourteen. He says: "Jack Kerouac
died today." Not yet the era when, for him, obits turn too
personal, friends, spectral. But they all knew the Lowell High
football star, famous writer, infamous town drunk. Dad asks did
I know who Jack Kerouac was? Too proud to say "No," I say,
"I've heard of him." Then dinner. Hamburger with a folded-up
slice inside it of American Cheese, soaked in tomato sauce.
Hot scoop of canned beans. Unaware as we were of any
meandering ghost.

*

Jack joined Gerard, saintly sibling, bed forever emptied
in 1926. Bed a créche. Creation knelt before a French-Canadian
messiah, that foretime before a flood filled the church basement,
before the great tree howled in the hurricane's lash. Gerard, the
truer Christ, never to be crucified, the boy become in eternity

the keeper of all the details ever forgotten on the earth. In *Visions of Gerard*, in lachrymose splendor worthy of Counter-Reformation devotional literature, the fire of a private sanctity consumes grieving.

*

Kerouac's Lowell novels are the cosmos of my parents, of my aunts, uncles, of all their friends, of the Depression, of the war years, of a mill town once flush, now dwindling, the textile trade fleeing to North Carolina. Prosperity withdrew like the breath of spring from an iced-up riverbank. Somewhat dark, somewhat Satanic, those emptied out mills. A downtown billboard with the greens, yellows, and reds of cigarette ads swabbed by rain into a greyish pulp. Massive, in peeling colors, a patent elixir Parousia. In hills and valleys around these rivers, an anthropology dissertation of interconnected clans. Not enough poverty to drive people out, not enough wealth to entice anyone in. A post-enlightenment technological Dark Ages. Flocks of kids driven into the pen of the one high school, then returned to the pastures of their ethnic villages. Portuguese, Irish, Greek, French, Poles. One girl in my old neighborhood – later in life a hospice nurse at my mother's deathbed – I remember her in her teens, cute, athletic, long black hair, stepping up to a diving board in summer. When she married, she moved fifteen minutes away, to another hill. A few years later, she moved back. "It was just too far."

*

Look up from a book of his and see on a clear afternoon: the crashing of rivers, the Concord and Merrymake, redbrick shimmering, foul, lucid pools, canals black and still, descending ranks of social prestige down to the river. The river itself, the flatness to the west. His prose set this city like a memorial candle in the currents of a century pulling away faster and faster from it. His immediacy was not what I felt or saw; it was the ascent of what I felt or saw into writing, the world taken back into heaven by words. But it was also, at times, what Kerouac called "the Greek tragedian nights of Lowell." The snowball fight in *Maggie Cassidy* in a downtown square, outside a restaurant, big clock in front of it, that was the restaurant my grandfather bought after his time in jail. In that restaurant he raffled off nylons for the war effort and snuck out to play the ponies. Long after the place went broke, we ate off its plates. Reading in *Maggie Cassidy* of the nineteen forties, of those in high school then, my uncle might be working the register, my mother might be at the pastry counter, flummoxed in her figuring out change for a bag of cookies bought by a woman hurrying to catch a bus. Her best friend, Joanne, behind a counter, saying something brilliant and pithy. Vanished ancestors crowd Kerouac's description but don't enter. Their lives are annotations of a page, a paragraph not in the book. They live in a Lowell long gone, while I sit here in the sun in California, yet the beauty of his lines keeps distracting me.

*

Leaves quiver in sunlight. A junk mail flyer has found its way onto the porch. Parts of the new answering machine are set out on a kitchen table freshly covered with a new blue and white flower pattern from Payless. Scent of new plastic. Multilingual instructions laid out before me in my bafflement. Then news comes from the East. News finds me, even here, at the edge of desert ringed in mountains, in jubilant heat. Now my heart's torn up. Tony's dad is dead, Mike Sampas, is dead shock of black hair, too thin to be in old-time movies, his eyes, ghosts of grief in their deep. My mother had a crush on him in high school. Father of six. Ramshackle barn packed with spare parts (but for what?). Patriarch who pronounced the First Noble Truth of Lowell: *You can't get blood from a stone.*

*

The 1930s, the old YMCA, heat pipes paint curling, chlorine wafts through every room, the dark parlor, men's pool table, no kids allowed, dark green walls, smoke, newspapers, at the foot of the stairs, the barber shop, the counter for hot cups of canned soup, the gym, the eternal chill, river wind filling all that's gone, train station, gone, opera house, gone, ancestors, gone, mills dilapidated, dark, vacant, the dead railroad tracks, last stop an alley, *Harvey's Bookland* that sold comic books, westerns, and, in back, porn, gone, *Three Copper Men*, its handmade sign:

PLEASE DO NOT TOUCH THE DANCERS

gone, the offices of *Donahue and Donahue*, the *YMCA* itself, torn down, adolescent boys milling on the steps, smoking cigarettes, then inside, routed into regimens, bumper pool fistfights, soda bottles, vending machine pizza slices, the humiliation of swimming naked, the fat coach in his beach chair, sadistic beside the steaming water, Saturdays a Three Stooges marathon, all of it is gone. In memory it's always twilight, always winter, downtown streets and storefronts always vanishing, boys always walking the miles home. And in the caged-off YMCA weight room off-duty cops are always lifting, some among them divers always pulling dead bodies from the river, any of it an outtake from a screen version of my years there, a French film called: *The Agony of Provincial Life*, or maybe a comedy: *Not to Die a Parish Death.* Wherever I am now or will ever be I'm on a bridge over the Merrimack in winter, but also, I'm gone, ends of my hair frozen crisp, walking back from swim team, watching currents twist under the ice, in the eternal twilight, and ahead, the long hill.

PASSAGEWORK

Here each lost breath
argues continuance, here
silences are linked & melodic.

A singer imitates grief because
there's no lament without song:
as in the old *Paint and Powder* shows of

childhood, there in the cavernous cold
beneath the old high school where the unlikeliest of
Carusoes astonished you.

And Mrs. Poznik vamped & pouted,
& Mr. Droney hurrahed with shillelagh across
a miserable stage more miraculous than Christmas.

Formulaic jokes, local names woven in . . .
There in the dark a boy flushes with pride
as his mother sings a song,

that crystalline pitch half a lifetime
of work, the copybook of breath exercises,
the triplets of dead masters ever in the ear,

Lily Pons, Claudia Mutzio, their legends,
bricks placed on a girl's diaphragm, all events
bending to the intensities of a song

which will resurrect the soul from
within the living death of the untuned body.
Exacting counterpoint of breath & blood . . .

How was it such masters quit
those lower orders of expression
& became pure spirit?

And so now doesn't it seem simply fair
that the angel of the voice should return to her
after many years and take back some breath?

It should not be trouble to understand that
a singer is asked to give one lung back to the void.
Music will not forsake her. Each song

has scored within its most
enduring moments countless other
truths which now in the silence of her

recovery, she hears, though not
without pain, like a new cadence, this
the passagework of the invisible.

IRISH TONGUE

i.m. Joanne Carpenter

Looking up one
evening from the
New York Review
of Books, remarking,
drink in hand, aside
the cigarette, eyes
dark, black, testament
she'd say, a beached
Spaniard in her
ancestral past, she,
looking up briefly
from the page,
apropos of what
never to be known,
eyes drop back
so as not to forecast
the shock of the thought,
her composure always
part of the shock
of whatever
Joanne said. In
this instance,
merely, "Nietzsche
was right!"

*

My mother's term of
highest admiration

one not unmixed
with wariness,
but always expressed at the edge of
some remembered hilarity
nothing even she
with her formidable
gift for impersonation
could do justice to
except to say:
"Let me put it this way:
Joanne has an Irish tongue."

*

Years later now
and both now dead
I remember
her Irish tongue
putting all to shame
with her brilliance.
Her most withering,
uproarious asides:
works of Irish art.

*

When I was a boy
coming up the beach
from the waves,
shivering towards the
stack of towels,

Joanne would have
just appeared, making
some killer remark.
I remember the
adults would all be
doubled over,
laughing.

AT NEWPORT

A thin woman in black flips over a shovel.
The dirt hits the wood of the casket
carved with the star of David. "Bye, Dad."
And afterwards, along the cliffs
at Newport, looking at mansions,
then out at the sea. Gentle
undulation, crumpling water,
light falling on the sweep of
houses across the bay.

NOBLE GHOST

Him, then, busting out a bunch of
Greek words, *hubris, arête,*
hamartia, anagnorisis . . .
We wrote them down.
They made no sense.
Seemed ridiculous. Then,
the course deepening, into and
through Aeschylus, Sophocles
and Euripides, we saw
those Greek words at work
all around, in life, in
dreams, in the news.

I see him amid all that
astonishment, being just
himself, hot-tempered, droll,
perverse in his musings,
startlingly candid.
The effect of reading
King Lear, sublimity
shot down through him
from his brains to his balls.
Each "never" sent a shiver
as a sign of some ever-
unfolding terrifying
teaching about grief:
the future dies inside us,
bringing a dismay at life
right down and into
to the very organ
meant to produce it.

I remember him
remarking, right there
in his kitchen, rung round
by wife, young daughters,
and his dorm proctor,
"The sole recompense
for embodiment is
coffee, sex, and cigarettes."

And at the end of the term
The Temptation to Be,
The Savage Mind,
The Seventh Seal,
and *The Divided Self* . . .

No compelling
case to kill yourself,
he might have said,
until there is. Then
young, diagnosed,
in pain, done with life,
he started up his car,
sat in his garage
and didn't go
anywhere, until
he did, until he went
back into the night,
the night before all nights,
back into the unknown
of which he had
revealed so much.

HEROIC DOLDRUMS

PURPLE RITUAL 1

heroic doldrums I

Orestes varied his pastimes. He had a taste for determinism and narrowed his leisure reading to Calvinist sermons and tabloid murders. Orestes was Irish. How else turn thirty and still be in flight? Still, he resisted seeing a shrink. He walked the shore at evening. He took in the bright sails of windsurfers, the luff and billow of the roped-in soul. He felt cruelly haloed by the sun god.

What analyst condones such a quest? A passing amour had remarked: "Hey honey? I've noticed you don't talk much about your past." He talked about his past. "Hey honey? You need help." He read idealist histories, mystical testaments. Made plans to hang himself, then glimpsed some grand shape of which his life was part, then began wondering what the shape was like apart from how he glimpsed it.

Orestes loafed. He prayed to Apollo. In honor of Malcolm Lowry, he drank mescal. The initiation he barely sensed was in fact underway. This was, then, albeit deeply concealed, a prime trial: that he admit the Furies were in earnest, the crime from long ago was ongoing, and that he come to see the implications. But of what, he could not quite remember.

family history

Images from before my birth, images of the New England of my parents, have greater clarity and force, for me, than images from my childhood in Texas.

A car decked in streamers. Tin cans. Apostrophes in shaving cream. I see the black suit of my turbulent grandfather, late in his failing. I see, that is, wedding photos. They left from the reception. In 1953 my parents began their southern descent, their Dixie diaspora, in a blue Plymouth, in 1953.

The assassination of John Kennedy was a metaphysical conceit worthy of Donne. Massachusetts and Texas, yoked by violence together.

Catholic. Northern. The assassination confirmed our strangeness.

heroic doldrums II

Orestes knew that the language of his inner life involved laws. And why would laws be needed, unless there were a conflict, some all-instigating mayhem? Which then came first, the conflict, or the law? Was there a first law, a commandment of conflict, so that another law might redress it? Did that first law stipulate its own violation as the terms of its fulfillment? Or was it, as he reasoned, conflict was the law, a law that was no law, and the latter, belated laws, mere repose. As this cottage by the sea was a repose, with its fresh coat of blue paint, its sprigs of basil and spearmint, its dissolving crests of seafoam visible from the breakfast table.

a sept ans

I note about my childhood: I was in Dallas when Kennedy was shot. Against this single afternoon, other afternoons might merit attention. But other afternoons seem aimless. Nothing to tell. Or they dwindle into shameful fantasies of flight and stealth, or into childish torments of acute self-consciousness: Naugahyde couch, white, late afternoon. Out the bay window, storm clouds. Or is it the sky turning purple before an onrush of storm clouds, above the neighbor's roof, itself white. I have just learned, am reciting to myself, the word "comfortable." The ease of the meaning of the word gets unsettled by its repetition. The sky, black and violet. The room, unlit. The accented syllable (the first? The second?) elusive. I wanted to own that word, "comfortable," but the fluctuation of my chant kept it from me, even in the moment of its utterance.

heroic doldrums III

Neither lawyer nor linguist, Orestes admired anthropologists. He fancied himself in far-flung rain forests, awarded some indecipherable kinship, bearing out to the world of glossy magazines the fundamental phobia. No lesser employment was acceptable. Unless it was this profitless pastime: scraping and painting the hull of a sailboat. Barnacles and wood rot excised; aqua blue paint smears the spiffed-up keel. But what would be the name of the boat? And, after so many summers at his lathe, or with flashlight and hammer, tapping at the interior, would the boat bear up on the ocean? And what islands or insights would the sun god lead him to, in this restless expiation, that fiery gold chariot rising from mountains under the sea, the crest of the helmet, the brilliant equipage of the horses, the light of which woke him, each morning, in his bedroom facing the sea.

stars and bars

From biographies of Southern heroes written for children, I conjured fantasias of fratricidal war. My devotion was to failed strategies and speculative histories. Even more than a confederation of modern Southern states, I dreamed of an independent Texas. A line of cowboy kings, from Sam Houston to, newly elected, not yet wounded, John Connally, a man not yet anointed by fate to live a long and public life aware of the silent grievance of multitudes of onlookers: *Why aren't you dead instead?* I had a grey Civil War cap and a cheap toy sized Stars and Bars. I secretly packed them on a trip back north. I astonished my Boston relatives. But my aunt and uncle betrayed my allegiance to Dixie. They secretly borrowed my hat and flag, to wear and wave as a joke at a cocktail party.

Purple Ritual

"Purple Ritual" is a portrait of Lee Harvey Oswald. The painter Ed Pashke reprises Oswald's pose from the Warren Commission: with rifle. In his backyard. In May. A pistol strapped to his waist. Furled newspapers in the hand free of the rifle. Printless, white paper. The kind you might wrap roses in. The Warren Commission identifies these papers as *The Worker* and *The Militant*. Combined, they have the heft of the *New York Times*. The white fence, or gate, the shrub to Oswald's left, the stairs and support beam to his right, are gone. Suburban bliss. The wife takes a break from hanging out diapers on a Sunday afternoon to photograph the assassin, her husband. Across the photo, a veil of purple. Oswald does not seem averse to the stars and stripes, or the four angry eagles guarding the corners of the canvas. Each clutches a shield in its claws.

my shirt

My brother gave me a T-shirt. Red body, white sleeves. More a jersey than a T-shirt. Sleeves, three-quarter length. Black letters across the chest: *Native Texan*. There is a red star in the arch of the second *a*. My brother had just returned from Dallas. The only one of us to return in the twenty years since we left. There's tension now in Texas, he says. Those born there take offense at those who move there and claim to be too quickly Texan. Were I to return, he says, I could be like a prophet! I could get honor in my own land! I love the shirt, but I wish the shirt had a cartoon cowboy with a bright yellow hat, like the one I got when father and son joined The Huddler's Club, a booster group for the Dallas Texans, a fledgling football team with the dullest name in the sport. The Cotton Bowl was immense. I remember the debris of other games littering the half empty rows, stomping on paper cups as the team battered away on the bright green field below.

my shirt II

The shirt my brother gave me I wear in Manhattan. I am a man from Massachusetts living in New York, wearing a *Native Texan* T-shirt. It's frayed, fading. I feel fated to wear it, perhaps through some lingering need to betray my conflicted origin. As when her lilt broke in on my reveries, at twilight, just as the shops were closing and the tempo of the street shifted into evening. "Wut pahrt of Tayxas are yeuh frohm?"

I meet JFK

First working for JFK. in the senatorial race of 1952 my uncle followed JFK to Washington as a White House aide. For Christmas that year, we received a large color photograph. My beautiful blonde Swedish aunt, my uncle, their six children grouped around the President. The children all had light, gold hair.

The portrait had a place of prominence on the mantle, and in my mind's eye. As schoolyard allegiances in Dallas trended toward Nixon, I told no one. My secret pride in my glittering cousins hid within it an envy. I wanted to be standing with them in that Kennedy nimbus and be dissolved in that glamor.

I'd been sent north that summer, after the birth of my brother, for a grand tour of family outposts. Handed off, aunt to aunt to grandmother to aunt to other grandmother to more aunts. I kept meeting relatives I never knew existed. At the end of this initiation, a last, notable stop. An evening awash with crowds, wavering with banners. Brass and kettle drums shook the cool Virginia air. JFK was on a dais, making remarks about the military.

With my cousins, the ones in the photograph, I waited for The President. JFK wound his way down the flagstone path. He paused. He greeted my uncle. My uncle then introduced each of the white-blond flock about them. Here, excitement dissolves the details. (But who forgets a first, radical upending of identity!) President Kennedy shook my hand and called me by my cousin's name.

casket

Not the bronze casket that he was first laid to rest in at the morgue, but a mahogany casket. The Kennedy family asked that the bronze casket be disposed. It was drilled with holes and dropped into the Atlantic Ocean, 130 miles off the coast.

rosa mundi

Over the years and the many trials, Rose came to understand herself as the sacrosanct feminine center of a world which included this world but was much greater. She knew she was sent to signify the abiding presence of the invisible. Her turning from this world heightened the fervor of the spiritual discourses that surrounded the Kennedys. The intensities of her inner life deepened.

the language of the spirit

Throughout the Kennedy Era, a Manichean war raged below the surface of all appearances, and this war was becoming visible but also more covert, more hidden. The words of one realm seemed the only words truly fit to describe the other. During these tumultuous years, the spirit could only speak the language of the flesh, and the flesh could only answer with the language of the spirit. One could only speak truly by speaking the opposite of what was the case. Questioned by reporters about how the President endured the absence of his earthly spouse, the White House spokesman answered honestly with an astounding lie: "The President had an early dinner. He retired, said his prayers, and went to bed."

Kennedyana

The camera does not reveal or steal the spirit of its interest, it simply omits the image of it, leaving an absence. As a child I did not understand this, but I felt it. I still feel it, and I am still trying to figure it out. The sunlit photograph of my aunt and uncle and their blonde flock gathered in the White House foyer with a deeply tanned and convivial President heightened the emptiness of my life. When I think of the dazzle of photographic data about the Kennedys, with their much-discussed media consciousness, their live-in photographer, I see a vast abyss, a frothing Niagara in the national life, a vanishing cascade of images. I see an abyss no river can never fill.

Irish ancestors

Saintly fire, earthy yen – these allegorical attributes of Rose and Joe as they appear in the tabloid masque of our national life undergo an inversion of values. Each mirrors the other. The holiness of Rose acquires a glamor. The lechery of Joe becomes a Roman zeal for civic virtue.

When I weigh the more provincial contradictions of the spiritual and the worldly in my own Irish Catholic family, my maternal grandmother embodies both extremes to a degree that defies exegesis. A musically gifted young woman from New York, she sang and danced on Broadway in a show called *The Vanities* When tipsy, she'd tell how she had been flown to Hollywood for a screen test. It was a screen test for a movie of Peter Pan. She lost the role to a future star.

The bitterness of this lost role would turn her attention to much else in her life. She left the stage. She married a millionaire. The millionaire went broke. The millionaire went to jail. She found herself and her children in a mill town far from her people. She drank, had breakdowns, prayed fervently, and taught schoolchildren how to sing and put on talent shows.

Though a New Yorker, her faith was a peasant faith, marked, or so I want to believe by the heresy of Jansenism. This faith passed to my mother, from whom I drank in, along with simple nourishment, that ancient religious doctrine called *contemptus mundi*, the hatred of life.

Sometimes in her cups she would talk about her brother. He died when she was eleven. It was a summer. He'd gone swimming in the river. He got a cold. He turned yellow and withered away. She said he was the only person who had ever really loved her.

First Communion

I'm in a white jacket. I'm outside the church. It seems almost dark, but that may be just the camera. I look like I'm nervous. I'm turning away. What comes more fully to mind are all the other pictures, the ones that did not come out. The packet from the drugstore showed a grey blur broken up and dispersed through multiple shots. The camera was fancy, German, new. Neither of my parents knew how to use the flash. My mother was terribly upset. Nothing to show the relatives on the trip north that Christmas. She cried and cried. The failure of the camera, endlessly tragic. My grief on my mother's behalf eclipsed any memory I had or have of the sacrament. Perhaps she sensed that the blurred, still-born snapshots foretold how time would take me away from her, was already taking me away from her.

the Adoration of the Host at Christ the King Catholic Church

Behind the altar, immense, Christ, on the throne of the Last Judgment, world held in a wounded hand. But even that looming conclusion dropped into shadows during the Forty Hours devotion. The men of the parish knelt before a frozen solar pulse above the bare altar until the serpent of night fled into the purple of dawn.

heroic doldrums IV

The deaths and betrayals of national families had for
too long amused and troubled him. But here, amid his Orphic
intuitions, sunlight and depth brought more pressing news.
From the pleasures of purposeful work, a single image of his early
past. An unequivocal gift. How had he ever forgotten it? That
magnificence! That ultimate cosmogonic song! Hardly occult,
it nonetheless announced itself: *The World Book Encyclopedia*!
The sheen of paper, a snowfield; all knowledge, alphabetically
ordered! Diagrams, graphs, maps, charts, illustrations; occasional
coloration, as if it were a multi-volume, exquisitely printed travel
brochure, this rapture of pure facts, presenting at a touch of the
hand the glittering minerals of the earth, the distinctive grain of
timothy grass, the icons of world religions, armies, martyrs, the
habitats of fabulous beasts.

untenable

"American media noticed no problem in the mystical
realm. Nor did JFK or Jackie. Nor did any friends or advisers, nor
did commentators on the public school uproar. Nor did even the
center of the mystical storm, Mrs. Madalyn Murray O'Hair. She
herself failed to understand the 'trap' into which she led, or rather
directed, JFK. The President's position on prayer in schools was
untenable. Whether he knew it or not, JFK was impeding the
cosmic flow of devotion, up and down the Cosmic Tree, and then
ultimately back to the Godhead."

magic bullet

Among the many speculations coming to the attention
of those still curious about the final truth, yet to be revealed,

recalled on the deathbed of the last living witnesses, those who saw the blood that day, that Friday in Dallas, those who kept watch over the body, those last dying few whose revelations only now arrive, are we any closer to understanding the finding announced long ago, and in another language, by an investigator in Buenos Aries? This once new truth has yet to be fully fathomed by those in the Northern Hemisphere. Among the bullets fired from the book depository window that day by Oswald, one bullet was different, inexplicable, yet mesmerizing in its implications. A man named Borges asserted the bullet that killed Kennedy came from the True Cross. This bullet, he said, the fatal bullet, was made from a nail of the True Cross.

Oswald at the window

The thin, tensed lips in his every pic makes me imagine Oswald with his mouth taped shut. The tape I imagine is electrician's tape. An imposed, emphatic black slot, like those which censors placed on the porno pictures of my childhood Eden. Private parts inked out. Shredded, at the conclusion of their study, by the older boys, but still to be glimpsed, in pieces in the dirt behind the barn. The electrician's tape imagined across the assassin's mouth stifles the only words of Oswald's I remember: "I'm a patsy," and transforms him into yet another Angel of History.

On an anniversary of the assassination a journalist said the nation needed, in a dialectical sense, an Oswald to step forth. The vastness of Kennedy required the minutiae of Oswald: the paper bag that wrapped the "curtain rods" Oswald brought to work that morning, the borrowed clipboard with the forms left unchecked, Oswald's task that morning, the green blanket in the garage where Marina Oswald lived, that held the rifle, the gnawed-on chicken-bone. The fact of that chicken-bone deeply impressed me, as a child, in 1963. The assassin ate chicken just before the kill.

Oswald provokes a hatred that long precedes him, a strife at work since Hesiod, that jab to the ribs as the stalwart officer in a white cowboy hat looks on, as Ruby thrusts the gun forward, as Oswald opens his mouth, his funny bone blown to bits by the secret joke Jack Ruby has just told him. He, Oswald, broke the literal power of the President. He proclaimed the kingdom of the figurative. Oswald's was an inaugural act of spiritual imagination. The assassin creates the void in which the images shine. He is what precedes the first flash of light. At the window. Inarticulate, and errant.

self-portrait with crucifix

White light eats through the depths of the hall. Left border, a tree all glitter. Glass planets. Paper angels. The pine needles look irradiated. To one side the boy stands, pale, cropped. New Christmas pajamas. The bottoms red, the top white. The garish instamatic light makes the whole world look washed out. Still, enough survives that cheap flash to conjure up the evening bath, the feverish joy, the feel of the fresh cloth, the wild sleeplessness. The boy looks toward the tree, past the gift he holds out and up in his hand, an offering for the camera, the truest gift, a crucifix. The photographer is his mother. She is making a point. The dark, polished wood of the cross, the shining gold body of the god, gold bands at the cardinal points, the tiny gold scroll above the head, the halo on the head, also gold, as if Jesus were innately alchemical in his suffering. The boy looks bored. Compelled to hold the crucifix up. Compelled to concede that Jesus giving his life for all will always be the only true Christmas gift. But the boy is looking through or beyond the cross. Even at this age, maybe seven, his devotion is at best fitful, is already wandering away. The boy looks beyond the cross to what is propped in a white chair in the foreground of the shot. It's another gift, concerning which he struggles to hide his excitement. The boy cannot look only at the cross. He is dazzled by the other gift, the bow and arrow set on the white chair, wrapped in clear plastic. Though the boy is more likely to be thinking of Indians or Robin Hood, the bow is the sign of another god, Apollo. The boy would prefer to be holding the bow.

heroic doldrums V

Orestes having much to the displeasure of his ancestors avoided law school, his task would be, while remaining uncommitted to his own innocence, and with utter disinterest, whatever this polis was, to assemble his own a jury. Fate had hidden his jurors. He needed to find them. The cottage was an interlude. The case could not be made to the pull of the tide or wind blowing green water to froth. In fact, these were his witnesses. These were his defense.

PURPLE RITUAL 2

Lee adored the Kennedys.
Marina Oswald

heroic doldrums VI

Orestes moved among Jews. Might so literate an elect, he thought, be the ones to finally fathom the Irish? (Still, he resisted psychoanalysis.) Orestes: in New York, but not of it. The purplish metallic vault of the night sky called to mind the defamation of temples. His freedom was the freedom of night stars seen through a hole in the roof.

Orestes killed time at cultic cites, destroyed or not, or yet to be. He wanted to feel whatever beliefs were sweeping the region. Violence was, for him, the first sign of a greater life. Meanwhile, the emissaries of Earth's dream, sod's daemonic brood, still pressed him. Their rage rewarded him, who proved the son as heroic as the father, yet always and forever a son.

He fancied himself a forerunner, a herald, himself the envoy sent to announce the return of pre-Olympian tumult. For him, the only acceptable death blow would be one fashioned from extravagant and ancient executions.

Among Jews, as among others, he felt neither tribed nor untribed. Every new allegiance felt like a fresh murder. Perhaps there was a hidden order, a divinity from before all divinities, or was there one who arose after all others were over, a god yet to show itself. What force might transfigure his affront? What element?

Not land. Not water. Not air. Possibly fire.

RFK Rolling in California

Headlines each morning, like messengers in a Greek play.
I'm the paperboy. June 1968. Folded pages fly heedless from my
hand. *The Boston Herald.* Day's editions skid down the linoleum
of apartment foyers. They wham the metal panel at the base of
a screen door. Unlike a messenger in a Greek play, I am utterly
unaware of the world.

Early light. Green branches dipped in gold. Deep rifts,
in the realm of the living: upheaval, writ large. Did I know
Robert Kennedy was dead *before* I returned to the house from
my morning paper route, delivering a headline that was already
outdated, no longer the story of the hour, the hour of his death
5 am, East Coast time?

The first way I remember it, I've heard the news. I
linger outside the house, not wanting to go in. The other way,
the primary win has me happy. I only learn of the assassination
getting set for school. My mother's scream fills the house. She's in
tears. She runs into my room and tells me: *It's happened again!*

heroic doldrums VII

Famous in shame, radiant in rage, comprehending, as he
did, the cause of all holocausts, embodying, as he did, the fruits
of reason, nonetheless, Orestes feared he was an actor baffled by
a sloppy script. Though unique, or so he believed, among Greek
myths, his transgression hid a simpler, more shameful offense:
flight from common life. For him, every new sanctuary was a dot
on a fabulous map. Maybe a fleck in an unchartered zone, amid
seas dyed red or blue or green, amid rivers flowing into endless
space, with lands conjured from bug-bored scripts, written-on
rags, dug out of the earth. His travels were blessedly distracting.

The water bright with high fire, the air earth-scented, no land in sight, the elements seemed to say he was unfathered, never born, free of fate, barely the breeze of a thought gaining knowledge of itself.

Imago Teddy I

Red, white, and, yes, blue, Teddy on the gallery wall. New York City, 1979. Andy Warhol and Kennedy children amid the convocation of contributors, drifting as did waiters with champagne. Deep into the evening, the expectation held fast: the Senator would arrive.

Midway through Ted Kennedy's presidential campaign my uncle decamped to New York. Called to revivify the foundering bid. His PT-109 tie clip made clear which brother brought him here. (Writing now, six years into the Reagan Restoration, how fantastic and grim is this moment.) Back in his element, full of élan, my uncle brought his fire to the room. Though a few years before he'd confessed, to an archivist at the Kennedy Library:

When he was shot, just my whole interest in politics stopped dead, cold, totally. What I used to do enthusiastically, I have never been able to do since. I can't get involved in it. I still know the things to do. I know how to do them. I know the way to do them, but I won't do them. And then when Bobby got shot, it was unbelievable. It just destroyed any idea I've had. I almost have a feeling now that if I get closely associated with someone, they're liable to get shot. An awful lot died that day.

Glitter across the tri-colored face of the Senator's portrait. My date, that evening, was a woman I had been wildly in love with for a year. We'd soon succumb to our own array of minor crises, separate, be miserable, live through much anguish, she, concussed, hospitalized, amnesiac, almost dead from cocaine, her memory only ever coming back in tatters, this night was before all that. No future ruin discerned by either. The romance of the invitation had us aglow. It let us hope for what a life together might be.

Behind us, looming, the face of absent Teddy, broad, diffident, never himself arriving, spangled with glittering specks by the pale hand of Andy Warhol. Face a knock-off of a knock-off, bodied forth from the silvery white of the surface through an application of black. The flesh of the lower lip implied by its shadow, the nose by gapped nostrils, then the crescendo of hair, the gaze averted, as if Teddy were tormented by guilt over Chappaquiddick.

This moment coincided with the peak of my new love's fascination with Buddhist thought. She looked at the portrait. She thought Andy had seen Teddy's awakening to samsara. Despite the glamour, festivity, and hope of the evening, Teddy seemed, in the portrait, to her, to be seeing beyond life. Within nonbeing, he looked down at the material world. He felt unsure he wanted to be born.

parenthetical fruit stand

(Talked till four. Your number, I immediately lost it. Over days, weeks, yes, months, I went looking for you. No one from the party knew you. No one knew your last name. No one knew where you were from. No one knew how you had arrived at the party. Many were moving away. Was that the party, a farewell? Did I not know? Were you, too, heading elsewhere? Many said, they remembered you. Your bravura. Your brainy beauty. I would watch the subway near where the party was. Maybe you lived nearby. Had a job. Went to the job. Maybe on the sidewalk some instant I was there, you'd be there. I looked by the bank, looked by the library. Once, I saw you. On a street full of noise, I heard nothing. Aching to say your name, I fell mute. Wasn't you. Days darkened. Weeks fled. Months. I lost my sublet. I house-sat for Tiffany, in the Financial District, not far from the water. By five, all was empty. Didn't affect me. I was ghostly. Kept looking. Any place you'd be, I found myself. Held in mind your black tresses, your glance, the swirl of your white skirt, your saying, near dawn, as we parted, on the street outside the party, goodnight, your turning away, as you said, call me.

That you had wanted me to call you was, to be candid, unbearable. All that solitary summer, tending cats offended by my distraction, I bore it. I imagined a world where I had the wherewithal to call you. A full year. Your image burning in me. Our chat. Perhaps, after all, you just loved ideas. Everyone else drank and danced. Your deepest desire was, it seemed, to talk about ideas. I grieved. You'd moved. Must have. I rebuked myself. Like so many, you had left New York. Was I the one person at a going-away party that stayed? Was I the only one for whom the party was, without my knowing it, the destination? Perfect light. Early summer. An unrelated errand to your hypothesized neighborhood. Blinding street, the climb from the train. Otherwise consumed, a world steamy, devastated. Who was that long dead "I" who didn't know you? I was reborn as a wretch at a tomb, ashamed to be still so abject. Nothing was left of any life before the night I met you. Love did not just humble me. Love annihilated me. How worthless, rebirth! You were gone, never to be here again.

Then, you were there. At a bodega, mid the outdoor crates, in sunglasses, shopping, picking up, selecting, certain favorites of the fruits of the earth.)

Chappaquiddick, Mon Amour

We Gargans don't shit in our beds.

Remembering the pictures hung along the back hallway of the old house, I can see my father's face quite clearly. I see him as a college baseball player, as a naval ensign, as a young attorney. I see him in family portraits, in snapshots from the annual Christmas party. But the face of his that comes to mind now I only saw once, on television. It was a court reporter's sketch. My father was making a case before a judge. It was the summer of Chappaquiddick. The client was the man who threw the party from which the Senator left for the ferry that night. The client was also the man who came back to the tide-pool with the Senator, and who himself dove down towards the upturned car. The sketch flashed a few seconds. We were all at the New Hampshire shore that summer, the news on at dinnertime. My father spent summer vacation down on the Cape, working on the Kennedy defense. The sketch was expressionist, slashes of black. A pastel blue swirl, his suit. Bluster of flesh tones. Was his hand against his face? It was strange to see him so. The image felt stripped of the glow of my pride. Fleeting as it was, it set him before the world for all to see, in what many took to be an uncertain moral atmosphere. His client was not even a Kennedy, but a Gargan, a cousin asked by Teddy to take the blame for the girl's death. That night the Senator sat bereft on the ground, his head in his hands, so went the account. Inside his head the tide-pool was a whirling grave; he seemed to himself as Blake might have painted him, terrified, aghast, fleeing the vortex, whereby knelt the weeping parents of Mary Jo Kopechne. Or so I now sketch it. I am ashamed to say that what I most remember is not the national drama unfolding day by day. What I remember is the advantage afforded by my father's absence from the house. One evening my cousin Timmy and I stole a beer from the fridge. Tasted it, didn't much like it, poured it out to foam in the sand in front of our summer rental.

Imago Teddy II

   Tousled, as if newly arrived on these shores, as if a
singer at the crest of the British Invasion. The neck brace,
zany sixties formal wear. As if the Senator were an extra in the
Magical Mystery Tour. Not quite a fifth Beatle, but other than
a fourth brother. In either case, an elusive identity. When an
older Kennedy dies, the other brothers move up a step on the
great ladder of ambition. Jack becomes Joe, Bobby, Jack. Teddy
passes muster as Bobby. But no one's there, where Teddy was.
Teddy fears he is only the avatar of one still on the way, the final
child, the Omega who ends the fret of what the family will be.
In the karmic cycle of the Kennedys, Teddy relives the fate of the
firstborn. He fell from the sky. No war sparked his aerial mishap.
Aloft in a private plane, Teddy dropped in an orchard. I imagine
the plane held in the arms of the earth, mangled in the branches
of an apple tree.

Imago Teddy III

   Death's wheelman. He who drives, then dives. He who
brings oblivion to the living. He who must descend, return to
Earth's womb. He who fails the living but keeps the dead alive.
The Senator was a chthonic candidate. One gloss of the scene
reveals Mary Jo is Teddy's relation to himself, is his own soul,
trapped in the back seat. Another, alert to nuptial imagery, calls
the wreck a watery wedding night. Beatific, the eager groom
swims down to gather the shy bride. Some elucidations of the
mystery slight Mary Jo in a rush to set Teddy among his brothers:
Joe is the will, Jack the intellect, Bobby the heart, Teddy the
body. But the fourfold fails. Teddy is too complex. On that
apocalyptic night his actions are the interplay of the brothers
within him. He is aware of himself as ever always only an aspect
of himself. Joe, Jack, and Bobby are partial manifestations of

his nature. Some scholars counter that the Senator remains unknowable to himself. Others, that the Senator must be seen as the occurrence in time of an otherwise unknowable Mary Jo. Many say that Mary Jo's death was Teddy's second birth. One Teddy dove; another Teddy rose. His pre-taped speech about Chappaquiddick says nothing so much as: "I alone emerged from the waters of night. I am beyond cause and effect as you know them. I am reborn."

heroic doldrums VIII

The oracle told him: set foot nowhere, not capitals or barren coves, only cream-colored beaches. Fate surged in the waves. Orestes felt new confusions. The dreams seemed real. The oracle said: hide. Said: fly. Said: your odyssey can never be written. Orestes fled evermore defiled through regions of purity. The oracle said: go to the land of the dead. Orestes sailed to Ireland. But there was no one there.

a pearl of great price

The many dives taken into the harrowing dark of the tide pool by the distraught Senator compose a manifold event. Each dive that night was distinct. Though none resulted in saving Mary Jo, each dive was uniquely fruitless. To see the dives as a singular, as a failed attempt to pull a woman from a submerged car, would be to simplify the Senator's fundamental nature. Each dive was its own incarnation. What the Senator groped for, the object of his truer inquiry, kept changing, kept showing him a new aspect, new again with each rise to the surface, each gulping breath, each slow turning of the body downward, into lightlessness.

interior paramour, final soliloquy

"It looked as if she were holding herself up to get a last breath of air. She didn't drown. It was a consciously assumed position. She didn't drown. She suffocated in her own air void. It took her three or four hours to die."

no coconut

No carved cry, no rescue scratch, no coconut coordinates for this sinking. Teddy's element was never water. The tide pool rebuked him. Every twelve hours protean Jack flooded in. In future years, the Senator, adrift in daylight, won heartfelt derision. His party boat was no PT-109, no "workhorse of the Cold War destroyer navy," as was the ship named after his firstborn brother. The Kennedy catalogue of ships ends, almost ends, with a tipsy holiday sail: an intoxicated Mayday on the rocks off of Hyannis. A foundering, mid-afternoon booty call. "Want to know why Teddy ran aground?" a Boston columnist joked. "His compass got confused by all the empty beer cans."

heroic doldrums IX

Orestes admired the pre-Socratics. He thought about atoms. Perhaps there is never any story but what they tell. Orestes, too, believed we're bound together for a flash of time, then nothing. He believed this is the only real history, the one always about to be blank. Orestes wondered what atoms ruled his states of feeling, what atoms created the illusion of a past. Had it ever mattered, who he was or is? Was the waiting just for nothing again to be? Between these two nothings, the nothing before and the nothing after, Orestes took comfort in asking, what nothing could ever be known for sure?

heroic doldrums X

Or was Clytemnestra just the gate of the invisible
shutting behind him, an agonized spasm through which
a soul reenters the world, forgetting one lifetime, learning
another, so as to assure the bliss of again forgetting. Orestes
sensed he'd never be exonerated at the temple of Apollo,
unless the temple was an infinite stretch of water, or piled
rocks where local ghosts flared over a whirlpool. At times he
felt he was becoming, of all things, abstract. As if he himself
were the hermeneutic god, and so lacked a guide downward
to the darker kingdom. He feared he had never been truly
polluted, and so he was never to be truly purified, was never
to authentically weep or exult, was never to be swept beyond
understanding, and into awe.

Live Peace in Toronto

A singer shot dead. Depression stamped our grief
on our brows, then cut us loose. The singer, whose melodies
were often enough death's echo, became our guide to a larger
and more deeply hidden Dakota. Lennon's wit, his caustic,
heartfelt push-back against fate, his death, were the telling of
yet another epic, one the lovers were in without knowing it.
His was an assassination just for them. They were walk-ons in
an Orphic mystery, each gesturing towards the other, but with
eyes averted. One of the records they loved was *Live Peace in
Toronto*. Before Lennon was shot dead, in the euphoria of their
first living together, they would put it on after dinner, drink
more wine, and dance around to "Dizzy Miss Lizzy."

heroic doldrums XI

Keen to die, be a ghost, Orestes felt shaken awake.
Turning sixty, yes, but hadn't he just been Odysseus in a dream?
Hadn't he lived a full life elsewhere than the basement of a
derelict temple? Or did he wake to find he was an Oedipus with
no daughter to lead him to a bright grove? Though dead, in
dreams both parents were delightfully benign. They didn't care
about earthly life anymore. They were beyond prophecy, beyond
rage. They were free of each other. Orestes was puzzled. His life,
almost over, felt yet not begun. Despite fear of the Furies, he,
too, felt free. He felt he was on a boat where those he had long
ago known mingled with faces never seen, some quite beautiful.
None more so that the one who recently appeared in a shroud of
flames, reminding him what a wreck he had made of love, and
done so in every dimension of his life.

heroic doldrums XII

In a painting his mother lay stabbed in the heart,
the knife blade visible above the very breast that had nursed
him. She was fleshier than he remembered, as were the Furies
who scourged and pierced the naked, fleeing man history
took to be him. The painting was of an age when to be flayed
by voluptuaries was glorious. The painter had given them all
ravishing bodies. Pain and nakedness were the final heroic
adventure. Even his recently diagnosed anhedonia seemed
alleviated by such art. The three Furies might as well be the three
Graces; he would give a golden apple to the one he best loved.
Perhaps the one with the lash. Which one was she, the bashful
one who might open his flesh directly to the sun, so that he

could, in advance of the cut, feel the elation of such punishment, the endorphins freed from the dark basement of his body? She, who would be his most vehement tormentor, his truest love.

heroic doldrums XIII

While never so curious as to pursue the question, nonetheless, for the better part of a life the kinship of two words, their apparently shared etymological blood, linked them in all his considerations of either, whenever either *consciousness*, or *conscience*, came to mind. One word conjured the other. To be aware was to be so of a thought, or of an act under deep suspicion. However much he dreamed of *consciousness* free of *conscience*, each was just a momentary forgetting of the other. It made no sense, that *conscience* should be the antithesis of *consciousness*, but that was what it felt like. As if, in a seizure of *conscience*, the exterior world darkened. The senses were burned to ash by the fires of recollection. Orestes considered that *consciousness* first awoke in response to *conscience*, as if the first feeling was to feel bad, but he could also imagine the opposite was the case. First came *consciousness*, boundless, ecstatic. Then, through mishap, misunderstanding, or error, *conscience* appeared, and all became woeful flight, as from an open grave.

RFK Rolling in California II

Out of the night, two angels appeared at the kitchen doorway of the now vanished hotel, to welcome the Senator into eternity. Each angel bore a gift in honor of that victory, that farewell, that death. One angel held a handgun. The other, rosary beads. These two angels came from afar, one from Palestine, the other from Mexico. They came as shining emissaries of those places, two different mansions within the palace of God, to the

Ambassador Hotel for the moment when God called his servant, Robert, home. RFK's leave-taking ceremony had two parts: the presentation of two gifts, one from each angel to this man who loved the poor, walked among them, his shirt sleeves rolled up, momentarily to be glorified. One of the gifts was a rosary, for all the novenas he would soon have time to say in eternity. The rosary beads would be a comfort pressed in his hand when the harsh, otherworldly light fell on him, on that kitchen floor, fell over his torn-up form as with his dying words he worried about others. ("Is Paul ok?") But the rosary given by the angel Romero is the second gift, a gift that could only truly be treasured after the presentation of the first, the gift given by the angel Sirhan. This was the angel Sirhan's first time among mortals. He was stunned to find himself embodied. He was distracted by the celebration. How strange it felt to have a hand and hold a piece of metal. The angel Sirhan meant to slip in and out undetected. He just wanted to get done what God had asked of him. God said to give the gift and be gone. But the angel Sirhan was new to Earth. Handing the gun to the Senator he gripped the handle and not the barrel. God had merely meant to lend the senator a pistol for personal use, to bring with him to the Holy Land, so he could shoot Palestinians, because in sending jets to Israel that was what he was doing. But the angel Sirhan mishandled the hand-off. Some say he shot eight times. Others say, thirteen.

RFK Rolling in California III

Juan Romero knelt at the grave. He wept, prayed, begged. He had cradled the head of the dying presidential candidate, a man he idolized, a man who had welcomed him the day before when as a busboy he had delivered food to the senator's hotel room. The senator, despite the campaign around him, looked at Juan Romero, saw him with warmth, with compassion. The senator thanked the busboy for bringing them all food. Juan Romero believed RFK understood and loved Mexican people, Mexican people who themselves loved America and wanted to be there, who had endured much, and would come to know, in the years ahead, cruelty, indifference, and also success. For the remaining fifty years of his life Juan Romero felt terrible about that day. Standing beside Sirhan Sirhan in the turbulent kitchen, the senator shaking hands with the hotel staff, Juan Romero only saw the gun seconds before it fired. Dazed, the next day he went to school as usual. The senator's blood was still on him. Why did God put him there, put those rosaries in his pocket? Why in all the world was he the one called upon to ask Ethel Kennedy if he could press rosary beads into the dying senator's hand? In time God's plans often made sense, but this remained senseless. The angel Juan Romero said he would rather have been shot dead and had the senator keep bringing light to the world than be kneeling at a grave in the rain, begging for forgiveness and wishing to be gone.

"Robert must die"

Did the two men revisit that eventful night? Some say they went moment by moment over the encounter for the full three hours. (Of the prison visit made by RFK Jr. to the man who murdered his father, no record.) Others say the apocalyptic jostle in the hotel kitchen went unmentioned. Still others say Robert and Sirhan wandered into philosophical and spiritual terrains, Sirhan at one point recalling the fortifying power of writing things down, over and over, and Robert recalling being hustled in the night age fourteen to his father's deathbed. So many years later, the two sat in the prison visiting room, still incredulous. Each bewildered by fate. Some say they sat a long time in silence. Some say that RFK Jr. forgave Sirhan and blessed him.

heroic doldrums XIV

In the gravest of hours RFK quoted Aeschylus. Orestes was moved to hear words he knew so well uttered millennia later amid yet another national catastrophe. Those words spoken over vast periods of time and across oceans and cultures on the night Martin Luther King was shot were both dispiriting and consoling.

Ritual drama, Orestes was pressed by events to admit, proved, once again, the only real means to understand life itself. He had long thought as he wandered the world, temple to temple, that ritual tragedy was even more powerfully at work in worlds where rituals seemed meaningless. Hours like this, he was back in ancient Greece, the Tragedy Festival in full swing. Recently Orestes heard that RFK Jr. had gone to visit Sirhan Sirhan, that the two men sat in prison and talked for three hours. This would be too much, even for Euripides! A second assassination, he could see in that a mythic tale. But disputes about the bullets? Spats about trajectories? Yet again, a second shooter? Or Sirhan quoting Oswald, "I, too, am a patsy?"

Orestes could not evade a further question: wasn't he a patsy as well? And wasn't he, son of Agamemnon and Clytemnestra, a second shooter of sorts, killing the killer of his father? Following Sirhan, Orestes read up on Rosicrucianism. He'd heard how by looking at candles for hours Sirhan had attuned himself to the divine mind. Had RFK Jr. in his pilgrimage to Sirhan Sirhan found his own attunement to the divine mind? In those hours of taking, were guilt and grief lifted from each?

More and more each dawn came at Orestes like an assassin. Each night he discovered his wounds and wondered where the bullets went. At night in bed, he lay on the floor of the Ambassador Hotel with rosary beads in his hand.

visual horizon I

In the absence of a visual horizon, two organs inside the ear, the otolith organs, instruct the base of the brain in matters of pitch, roll and yaw. In a dearth of visual information these organs stir "illusory non-visual sensations." A pilot without instrument training flying a plane through fog over an ocean at night can be flying upside down without knowing it. The "drift in the inner ear" quickens. Errors in the feel of the perceived rate of a turn can occur in the brain at the rate of 0.2 to 0.3 degrees per second. The consequence is called a "graveyard spiral." (The pilot still believes he or she is maintaining a straight flight.) Once the visual horizon is lost, the average time for pilots untrained in instrumental navigation to persist in avoiding a "graveyard spiral" is one hundred and seventy-eight seconds.

visual horizon II

Inside the ear the two crucial organs stand at right angles to each other. One senses speed on a horizontal plane. The other senses gravity on the vertical plane. When the "graveyard spiral" begins, the brain cannot tell flight speed from gravity. John Kennedy Jr. flew his plane straight down into the sea at night. He surely believed himself level for a landing on the Vineyard. Without a visual horizon, no one on the plane felt how atilt they were. Not Kennedy. Not the two sisters in the back seat, facing away from him. Kennedy's sister-in-law had moved past her apology for the delay that made her late to the airport. Her sister, his wife, tweaked their appetites with news of the dinner awaiting them: grilled steaks and peach pie. The pilot, John, felt the decision to turn from the lit-up coastline, and head into fog over the ocean at night, was working out.

visual horizon III

In the annals of disorientation, John Kennedy Jr. is
not alone. The pilot who flew Patsy Cline was likewise addled.
Witnesses called that earlier infamous crash a muffled puff,
followed by silence. There are others. Aeroflot 821. Rather than
land, the plane tipped toward the sky. The pilot sounded "mildly
intoxicated." All died. The plane was found in pieces. The pieces
were on fire. The pilot who flew the Big Bopper to his death
surely experienced the vanishing of the visual horizon. (The
doomed Bopper said to Dion, Valens, and Richardson, "We're the
ones making money, we should be the ones flying ahead.") They
hit the ground at 170 miles an hour. (Autopsies failed to confirm
a gunshot.) Low clouds and rain brought down the Rama in
Queensland, Australia. Locals on motorbikes joined in the crash
search, as did, on horseback, police. All flyers died. Curiously,
age eleven, the pilot had survived a crash which had killed both
his father and his brother. A further curiosity: that plane, a red
biplane popular at Australian airshows, was also called the Rama.
Yet another believed to have suffered from spatial disorientation
found himself alone in a small plane. Thought he saw a craft a
thousand feet above him. He was also Australian, and a flying
saucer enthusiast. Were aliens toying with him? His last words:
"It's not an aircraft." Upside down without knowing it, some
conclude. He may have seen his own lights reflected on the water.
But others argue the "lights" were, in fact, the planets Venus,
Mars, and Mercury, along with the star Antares.

visual horizon IV

A well-known photograph. John-John in the Oval
Office. Under the Presidential desk, peeking out. John-John has
found a hiding place which gives him a vantage. He looks to
be fully in his own moment. The Free World wheels on above

him. Were the Cuban Missile Crisis to be going on overhead, he wouldn't know it. Whoever remembers childhood knows what John-John is experiencing. Whoever remembers when their bodies were smaller knows the exhilaration of a place that only he or she or they can get to. The other photograph, as public as this is private, but this is public as well, is only weeks away. Draped in black, pulled by horses, his father's coffin. John-John saluting his true father, death.

21 George Street

Mostly glass, some white brick and aluminum, built by two brothers. What the future would be, rising amid empty mills. The brothers built *21 George Street* to house the law firm started in the 1890s by their grandfather, an Irishman who lost an eye working for a butcher, then got himself a law degree. This cube from the future was built with bucks got in Dallas in an oil deal: derricks off the coast of Scotland. All that glass and metal gleaming in the sun gave descendants and relatives of the two brothers a local eminence. *21 George Street* could have been lowered down from the sky, so proud you were of it, that architectural extravagance, dreamed up in a world where there would never be an oil crisis. Heating bills stacked high. It was a struggle to keep tenants. In the end, the only tenant was the great patriarchal firm itself. The white brick, the reflecting windows, decades later there was still nothing like it in Lowell. It shone throughout your youth. In sixth grade, atoning for your inattention in math class, you'd pass it walking home from summer school, and stop and visit, and get a quarter to buy yourself an ice cream soda at the drug store before the long climb up the hills to home.

21 George Street II

Great-grandfather, grandfather, father, uncle, brother, cousins, the shining square of steel and glass and white brick, you think you'll take your two young sons to see it, see their grandfather and uncle, see the family name on the door, see the younger, unrelated lawyers hard at work. For an hour your sons will see it, will share what was your world, your complex feelings for the moment settling into pride, pride, and love for all this office meant, for past and passing generations. But you didn't think to call in advance. You had let no one know. It was a Friday in midsummer. No one there but the secretary. You walked with your sons through the meeting rooms, past the file cabinets, the portraits of patriarchs, past your younger brother's office, where you stopped to leave a humorous note, though you were by now deeply sunk in sadness, there at your father's office, with his view of the Concord River.

heroic doldrums XV

Orestes often felt pressed to rouse enough energy to keep fleeing, searching for a temple which the Furies could not find. More and more he simply wanted the life that was before what happened, happened. He was puzzled by how little he remembered of it. In dreams he felt the presence of his parents, but seldom met them there. They were either just gone, or there, but hidden. Orestes's deeper dream, admittedly grandiose, was of a yet to be articulated system of thought proving all was otherwise. Orestes thought about Persia. He imagined a land beyond all he had known, a land where the fates available to scions of royal houses were not, he thought, excruciating. He would die here today if he could be reborn there.

I am a Kennedy

Struck with a golf club so that the club broke, so that the beheaded shaft of the club gave the murderer a second weapon, a weapon used to further stab the fifteen year old blonde neighbor girl he was sweet on, stab her in the neck with the lighter end of the broken golf club, the club having broken as he beat her with it, the six iron, a club with a loft angle of 31 degrees, capable of achieving a distance of 150 yards. In the reprieve of the leaves, she lay dead or dying. He had presence of mind enough to pull off her pants and underwear. No need for sexual violation. Her half naked was sufficiently fulfilling. In this long moment, Skakel became a Kennedy. A cousin by marriage, no Kennedy blood in his veins, he would, to a prison therapy group, nonetheless proclaim: "I am a Kennedy."

in a tree

That Halloween night, that Celtic festival of Samhain, he told the police he was elsewhere. Throughout the bludgeoning and stabbing and murdering of the fifteen-year-old strawberry blonde next door, he was, he said, nestled in a niche of branches, in a tree outside her bedroom. He was imagining, he told the police, her in bed in a nightgown in the dark and alive. He did not know she was not there, not there but semi-naked, bloody, dead, down below, in the back yard, where her body had been dragged. For the proposed time frame of the murder, he was, he told the police, looking at her darkened window and jerking off.

PT-59

With PT-109 sunk in the Pacific, Jack Kennedy was chosen to be captain of another boat, PT-59. With PT-59 he attacked Japanese barges. With PT-59 he crept up on and assailed shore batteries. With PT-59, in the northern Solomon Islands, he rescued ten Marines. (One, given Kennedy's bunk, died there.) The war over, PT-59 was sold off. PT-59 became a charter boat for weekend anglers, painted white. Its machine guns were swapped out for fishing rod holders.

heroic doldrums XVI

Orestes' sons came by to upbraid him. They pointed out what had not gone well in their upbringing. They said his infamy was an unamusing legacy. They wore ritual masks. Perhaps they were not even his sons. It was not impossible that Orestes had arrived in Japan and found a Shinto sanctuary. (Fanciful scholars would call him the founder of the Noh plays.) His sons, as was their wont, took up his shortcomings. They noted how far short he had fallen of their world-conquering grandfather, who had, after all, destroyed Troy just because he could. Though she was dead before they were born, they had tender memories of Clytemnestra. They brought those memories up. Orestes considered his sons sentimental and selective in what they remembered and did not keep this opinion to himself. A crowd gathered. Passersby mistook the visit for a ritual performance. His sons were beating drums between their dithyrambic indictments. He loved his sons, but he remembered their childhood no more clearly than he did his own.

the last Kennedy death

The lawn ended at the bay, so the ball bounded into the water and drifted quickly out. Without the ball the game could not be played. All were having much fun playing the game, so the young Kennedy mother and her son went out in a canoe to get the ball.

Wind blew in off the bay. Further out, beyond the shelter of the cove where the Kennedy summer house was, the waves got bigger. The Kennedy mother and her son did not know this, nor did any other Kennedy, or non-Kennedy, enjoying the Sunday afternoon. The current tugged the ball into the open bay. The Kennedy mother and her son paddled after it. Higher winds. Higher waves.

The theory is, during what was, onshore, just a break in the game, the canoe with the Kennedy mother and her son was overwhelmed. Some questions may yet find answers, others not. For example: did they drown together, or apart? Did son or mother see the other disappear in the waves, then live on a while longer, in the shock of that knowledge? One of the bodies has yet to be recovered.

heroic doldrums XVII

Orestes did not often think about why his life had been so unhappy. Had he only not killed his mother, he now believed, he would have been, would be, happy. Orestes felt he had been a happy child, before he murdered his mother. Something must have made him very mad. He must have felt betrayed, and he betrayed her. She must have made some impossible demand. But he wondered, now, had she really asked that much of him? All she had asked of him was a favor. All she had asked of him was that he believe in Jesus. How hard would it have been, to just say the Apostles' Creed? To just go to Mass. To just take communion. Had he granted that favor, he could have gone back to being happy. Instead, he murdered her. As much as murdered her. He rejected Jesus. He said, to her, before he murdered her, that he would never feel love for Jesus. His mother died knowing her son would never be the priest she had asked heaven that he one day be. Orestes missed being happy. He missed her being alive.

Ages since her death, he still, for a second, forgets that she's dead. In that second, he wants to call her up. He wants to tell her some funny thing she would like. He wants once more what she so loved: long, spiritual conversations. In that second, he wants just one more time to hear her talk about her day.

Caroline goes for a swim

> the daughter bears
> the coconut of life upon
> father-famed seas
>
> Albert Mobilio

Didn't you once in your childish heart imagine you would marry her, the sad princess of your once illustrious people, imagine you were the one, of all in the land, who could make her smile again, help her forget her father's horrible fate? So, so sad, what happened to her, who even in her sorrow had such lively, knowing eyes. Eyes all the world saw at the funeral procession, when the riderless black horse of death went by and her brother saluted and her mother was in black and all the uncles and her mother had a veil over her face as if she were in the underworld, having been swept there already by the Lord of Hades, Aristotle Onassis. Various weddings over many years happened. None were you and Caroline. If from a great distance, you have always thought of her fondly. You felt no bitterness when someone else stole her away. You have always wished her well in her adventures. Here at the other end of life she looks trim and attractive, in a blue bathing suit. Her son and some native tribesmen stand up to their waists in warm, glowing South Seas water, in the background, white sands and palm trees, she in that sacred water looking amazed, determined, half unsure if she is about to dive in or has just risen from it. As if finally, after a lifetime, she has returned to life, has demonstrably arisen from so many seas and inlets of death, like the one that took her brother. She seems happy, grateful, given that she is a Kennedy, to have had a life, to have given life to another, her son, there beside her for this historic swim. Mother and son are recreating the swim her father JFK made in 1943, when a Japanese destroyer sank his PT boat: middle of the night, cut it in half. The waters flamed. Kennedy led his men on a treacherous swim through the elemental maw to a small island. Once there, he wrote a rescue note on a coconut, passed on to naval command by helpful natives. These gentle swells are then the seas of life and Caroline swims in them. She reenacts the laps between islands that her father, once the captain of the Harvard swim team, swam in dire earnest, in search of food, water, rescue, and, yes, the laurel of war hero. (Though asked had he had planned to become a war hero, Kennedy responded: "It was involuntary. They sank my boat.") Caroline swims in her blue bathing suit with her son the very waters in which their common ancestor was immersed. (And what Kennedy ever emerges from the sea the same?) This was the dunking that gave her father a new life, and eventually a spectacular death. In her goggles his daughter dives in from the island now named after him, Kennedy Island, though the Russians call it Oswald Island. (And does Marina, named, after all, for the sea itself, secretly at night go for a swim as well?) Caroline knows that if she falters her father will save her. In the afterlife JFK watches his daughter swim the same waves he swam and feels she is saving him. So much is over for them both. Time to kick and twist. Time to splash. Time to enter the waters of rebirth. It's a refreshing frolic, the kind Kennedys of old liked to enact, in Hyannis and elsewhere. The water rushing by, now and then Caroline lifts her head from the water and checks the horizon. She's heading toward the island where her exhausted father once found fresh water and a tin of hard candy.

SHADOWS IN THE WATER

SHADOWS IN THE WATER

And other confines there behold
Of light and darkness, heat and cold.
Traherne

I

Glacial range
of harbor rock-salt

winter, weeks away
but looming in the chill –

spotlit gouge,
hoist & pour

(The ship a rust-bucket
dead in the water)

padlocked beach arcades
homes nailed shut

& a couple, thieving a box,
in the shadow of the crane at night.

Crystalline fire,
let nothing

outlast your
scattering

The whole grandeur
of the Atlantic's

a sullied heap,
a null gist.

II

Dress a trembling blue flame.
Delicate steps through the breach in the sea wall

glint
of gold,

her quick hand,
ring her sister left her,

cloud shadow falling across her face.
Willowy green scrub bending over hot sand.

Grieving fades & now
a thought wells,

a pulse of air,
an entangling

joy, nothing
can stop it –

not the silver flecks,
the perpetually rewritten

gospel of sunlight on water.
Not the monarch's wing in the white petals.

Not the drink in hand,
or bright vapor on the path.

Sunlight crosses an incredulous face.
The blue world seems threaded, now, with black.

Breach in the seawall.
Face to the glare.

As if beside her for
a flashing instant

the anorexic, her sister, who saw
Creation and turned away.

The moment opens
 all its gates . . .

Island, white horizon,
broken fields of black water.

III

Subzero. Nightfall. Alone,
driving back to a house

unlit on a point facing the sea.
Passing, then, a pond, ducks huddled,

forty martyrs on the ice,
no bonfires blazing

on the shore, bonfires
set, long ago, by the Emperor

to tempt the transcendent
back to this world.

They never were,
those times death in

the cold was life. Geese,
wings clipped, shriek.

Wind lays bare the yard. Burrs, scrub,
the stake that once chained a dog,

visible in the headlight.
Dashboard goes dark.

I'm home. Stepping
out. The phone inside

the unlit house
is ringing.

IV

Towels fouled by
guests, towels

like impromptu
tourniquets

for a brutal
wound,

or else, unfolded
in the wind by

a beautiful woman
at the beach, brushed

by the breeze
like the hair

she lets down
over her shoulders,

not to mention the
more legendary

ablutions: the hand
towel handed to Pilate,

the facecloth of
Veronica,

once grimy gnarls,
freshly folded,

radiating
dryer heat.

*

No reprieve
needed, these

keep insisting from the
heart of the

absolving
blaze.

*

Though should the ghost of
a smear

survive, as
can be the case

with fairway towels,
bar rags,

and, of course,
the bedding of

amorous
inebriants,

the launderer is
free to infer

the visible
betrays

the true,
the washed

but indelibly
stained is

no less clean
no less returned

to a primordial
purity.

                *

As a penitent
might feel leaving

a confessional
as a priest might feel

mid-Mass
washing his

hands
before the

elevation
of the Host . . .

                *

(Or like the wretch
in *The Inferno*

might feel,
no, felt, just

before
hanging

himself in the
doorway

of his
house.)

V

Brian was a farm boy,
strong & stupid,

a psychopath
who only

feared two of us:
Carl, a former semi-pro

halfback who won
a split scalp once, from

Brian's pool cue –
& me. (I wrestled

in high school.)
Brian & I had a game.

He'd fly at me any which way.
I'd pin him in seconds,

then press him into
the cold linoleum

(& those holds hurt.)
He was scared, angry,

and humiliated,
& he loved

playing
that game.

VI

Of D, agoraphobe, who
said: *The joy of others violates me.*

and of L, botched
by a doctor,

sex was "not out of
the question," she said,

but its pleasure,
for her, could only

be, she said, that
of a refugee

whose
kin

had been
obliterated.

VII

It was a deeply unhappy time in my life.
It was a time straight out of

The Varieties of Religious Experience.
A bright morning in early summer.

I was walking crosstown on 53rd
to my job at the astrology office

proofreading horoscopes.
I was just past MOMA.

Light grew less. On my left side
my peripheral vision vanished.

No real physical sensation
accompanied the semi-blindness,

save those resembling panic.
It was a racing arising less from

the loss of the visual field
than from a black electricity

welling at the edge of the eye
and then within the eye.

I felt a furious force
coming to be inside me.

Felt exalted and alert, and also,
a desire to walk into traffic.

The black electricity crackled
and sparked and roiled within me

for a block then trailed off,
as if my life was just

a momentary hole
through which some

energetic malevolence
spilled into this world.

VIII

A pale, almost gold
burning over

the visible
world, over

the estuary where
grit once spilled in shallows

the funeral boat
turning back

to the dock,
over the

grieving drift, the
cataclysmic shivering.

IX

Seaweed gleaming
in radii of ice.

Sunlight pouring, now,
over the leveling of

a house, upper floor
torn away, beams

gone, wires all
slack. Walls

all broken, the
bits, hauled away.

Room of the suicide,
a sky-blue cube.

X

Grand Tetons

Ravine, a long day dying in a flare.
Sunlight spilling gold

over the ice floe
canyon. Green plunge.

Char of a tree.
Hints glimmer

on a failing peak.
(A marten curls in sleep.)

This range is
dissolving.

The chapel at
the base is gone.

Gone, glorified body,
apostles falling

back. The burst
of beyond.

The visible
world

ceasing
to be.

XI

the Hector-body
Olson

The great epic of the Greeks
confers only

a passing majesty
on the blooded

hope the
demi-god

will haul inviolable
& dead around the city

Hector, whose
judgment & nobility,

at first so
glorified,

are now ridiculed.
Not bravery in the end:

bewilderment,
blood in the breeze like

the scent of
a distant river –

livestock
sense the doom –

the house of Priam
a reek of ruined bodies –

sky tilting, invisible
stars sliding,

the favor of God
turns to

the true
hero, death,

pitiless, magnificent,
arrayed in the sun's fire.

Only a brother,
beside him,

a sudden living
image sent

to deceive him,
offering to die

with him,
there, in the

billowing mist of
bright grit.

XII
Frank

Face, flush, then ashen,
fired first thing

Monday, the
sacked ad man,

a decade of
desktop clutter

cramming a paper
bag at his feet.

He's meekly seated
in the reception area,

by the door, amid
mementoes and

knickknacks,
a file or two, he's

close to crying,
his grown son's

coming to
retrieve him,

as career-long
colleagues

in the world of
illuminated

taxicab rooftop
advertising

arrive
for work.

XIII

Vince

Wife on the way
to repatriate his office

enhancements, pictures
with prestige clients

long on the wall.
The room is dark.

Out of respect for death
the shade is drawn.

I sit in his chair.
I see his daughter,

giving him a hug.
I lean back, swivel.

I see his drinking days,
the dead executive.

There he is with
Jake La Motta.

*

Sliced in the light of
the Xerox, in recent days

he'd hover in the
hallway, complexion

near ghastly,
copying,

whatever, for his
files, newsletters of

Marketing Research,
finance mags,

mock-ups for
Reynolds,

Tarrytown, one
last for

the guy in
the cowboy hat.

        *

Vince, then
joking: *I am*

*the original
Marlboro Man.*

XIV

after a painting by Tony Sampas

I am the burning field
glimpsed through

the aperture, and
I am the dark blur

that is your
vantage.

I am the deer
in the tapered mist.

I am present only in
absolute stillness,

present only in
dire trembling.

I am the lost soul crossing
a field at evening.

My helmet is green.
My face is hidden.

I am the guard,
poised and vigilant,

between plenitude
and privation,

between where
you are and

where you
are not.

I am that far-off luster,
a brightness that pierces stone.

I am the sunlit harvest
Tolstoy spoke of,

and the burning of
the chaff of earthly

vanities as grist
turns to spirit.

I am the guard
keeping you from

the field, the barbed tangle
beyond which the deer

call you to stand
among them,

at one with the mist
that rises from the river.

(Are there deer
roving in the harvest,

or are they just
further forms of

torment darkening
the final fire?)

I am only a guard who
keeps you in darkness,

less than a guard,
a gate beyond

which fulfillment
impossibly shimmers.

a broken gate, open,
beyond which

wheat stands unwinnowed
in a burnished space.

XV

The only sound
in all Manhattan

is of coming
and going.

(You're going,
I'm hardly here.)

    *

Click and whine inside
blackened brick,

the elevator's
block and tackle.

The Hudson glitters.
Weather-beaten

wooden water tower.
A hanging ladder

ends mid-air,
sixteen floors up.

    *

Heating oil
smoke puff

fading above
the furnace flue.

It's shadow
overhead

also
fading.

*

At last,
ecstasy ex-

hausts them,
too chafed

even to be
touched.

Far from bed,
they're in the foyer,

pale, pleasant,
and about

to part
forever.

One says:
"I love

you as much
as when we

first met." And
the other

jokes: "But
we are

hardly
such souls

as Love
saves."

*

Lovers are chaste
who never were before.

Billowing rain would be
your purple gown

but I'm waiting
for a bus in sunlight.

*

Have I ever walked
so barefoot across

so plush a carpet?
Green Persian

emblems
a wash of blue.

Plants shimmer
in sunlight.

Rooftop gap
between

grammar school
and warehouse,

midwinter blaze
pouring through . . .

Then you call
& say, "I can't

make it. Not
today. Not

tomorrow.
I'll call you,

but this won't
happen. I'm

leaving
New York.

I'm moving to
North Carolina.

I've enrolled
in a beauty school.

You'll never see
me again."

      *

I see the sky's
illuminated script

& the rinse that
sheens roofs

& windows.
Small hour.

Apartment empty.
Thoughts rise as

water falls.
Sword flash, match

flare, wet and vibrant,
diminution & surge,

rip & stitch,
a watery garment,

the silver I will
put on &

disappear,
a feathery vapor.

A legible light
comes close

but withdraws. To
touch the earth

would be to
burn it.

The gold glow
makes of

vanishing
a caress, makes

desire a
stir of

earth, air, and
miraculous fire.

XVI

The East seemed, as
after an eye exam, pupils

widened, a fierce
glare, all earthly

objects, painful
to look at.

*

But I intuited the temple, the stars, the planets
ringing the Christ who

guides the guide.
I saw, in my heart, in Utah,

the gathered facts of
all the dead.

*

An acquaintance came here
once, and traced herself

back to Edmund Waller,
to a regicide who fled

the restoration, to
a Duke with a cruel but

elegant solution
to the Irish problem.

*

A quick dip
in the Dead Sea,

a storm rising
in the foothills.

*

I see again the concentric
rings rippling outward

from Havana, the
newscasters speculating

how far the rockets might reach.
I saw and listened, my

Reason not yet
certified by

sacrament, by
First Communion

at *Christ the King* of
the pierced hand holding

the cross-topped globe
backlit by Byzantine shimmer.

Dallas flight delay.
I'm reading *The Kennedy*

Imprisonment,
but thinking about

a great ring of pure
and endless light.

The dark statesmen fly
up into the ring.

Kennedy and Castro
fly up into the ring.

Those dead in the Bay of Pigs
fly up into the ring.

Whole dethroned juntas
fly up into the ring.

Figures of accolade and
scandal rise through the spill

of stars and space debris
passing into the ring.

Mercenaries, missionaries,
slaves, tribal remnants,

utopians, fanatics
awaiting the final days,

the dim-witted, the brilliant,
boys and girls excited

by their first kiss,
fly up into the ring,

high above the airport
until at last, even

Cotton Mather, the
author *of Magnalia*

Christi America,
flies up into the ring.

XVII

Earth gouge, hollows, stone
dead cultures, blonde memorial

chunks, rattles, painted hides,
cosmologies, weapons.

Heat and silence. The dirt
prays: Permit nothing.

Only the moisture the
leaves offer up each day,

a dire dryness done in
 by a cactus flower,

by the touch of green
root tipped in fire,

a pent-up sweeping
through the evergreen

wedged in orange crag,
pressing toward red

vistas at sunrise. Galaxies
adrift in the night sky . . .

        *

That was the life he lived there,
that fellow Manhattan juror.

*

A murder kept us idle all week.
He, waiting each day, wanting

(the trial never happened)
to be back in New Mexico,

rapt in that transcendent
solitude. Water tins,

adobe huts, kiva
murals, gold seeds of rain

transforming the scorch
into nibs of green.

*

We, there waiting with him,
rapt as well, listened.

Rather than contemplate
that allegedly horrible death

we were elsewhere, in his
distant world, that

desert where thirst
is eternal, where

a cool sip feels
like endlessness.

XVIII

disfluency

The last words, or word, or
syllable of last

word, said, again, to
himself, seconds

after speaking, his
own words echoing during

the usual silence of
awaiting reply,

usually around
age five and

soon transcended,
Word Final Disfluency.

A quiet voice, a ghostly
second wave of

sense, sharp
clear sounds

having just quit the
boy's mouth

an intimate echo of
his words even as they

drift into your
understanding,

but hushed, the
plosives, fricatives,

the ululations of
vowels, as if,

for the boy
asking about the

TV show, sense
and sound

were coming
undone, only

opening of
any sentence

could be
counted on.

And so
he sounded to

himself, yet
again, the final

sounds, the omega
of his pronouncement,

its flight from
his mouth to

a hearing, as
a whisper,

feeling out the effect,
or fashioning

a spell to guard
and guide

words towards
some fuller

comprehension
deep inside

word's
end.

For the duration of this
deviance, any stray

utterance can be
erratically

liturgical. And
a parent hopes that

his innocent
barely heard and

fleeting
incantation

is only an impromptu
and unconscious

prayer to
Hermes,

the god of words
that come from

afar, that
the boy will

win a blessing and
fall silent as any

other oracle
might do.

So that this
novel devotion

not be revealed to be
the first symptom of

some ever less
coherent

rebounding of
sounds, some emerging

lifelong recursion of
the terminal, a

debilitating abyss
this emerging

consciousness, this boy
will abide in forever,

between sense
and echo.

XIX

(MRI)

The long humming tube is
not much like

the caves below
the Black Hills of

North Dakota,
the guide saying

now put out your
flashlights and candles,

up above us, the
darkest dark

still has slivers
of light inside it,

but here, there is
no possibility of light.

XX

A man told me: my turn will
come. He will lead me, he said,

blindfolded, to the cave of dreams.
Later, a girl gave me a paper cup

red with liquid: "This tastes like
water. It kills inhibitions, and

has no side effects." I wanted to
flow with it all, be part of it, but

I didn't know what to do next.
The room spun. Most were naked.

The musicians were like kids
beating a toy piano, but the

notes seemed dark, mysterious.
On the wall-sized video screens:

people in costumes, taking them off.
When, in the bathroom, we locked

the door, a man in black underwear
asked me to jack off all over him.

Later, with all wrapped in
cellophane, a woman told about

a wounded healer. She'd a story
about innocent, loving gods

on an island called Lila.
A blind girl played a flute.

They wheeled out a prophet
too mangled to speak.

When he sang, he wailed. His
twisted body cranked halfway

out of his chair. Wanting
to use words, he bent toward

letters on a tablet, waving
a pointer wired to his head.

The death of the old you
will not be painful, they said.

The death of the old you
will be gentle, like a massage.

When the old you truly dies,
they said, you will enjoy

a blissful floating in
the sea between lives.

XXI

She was my
adopted mother

but wanted
to be my

real mother.
The kiss

would've made
that happen.

She wanted a kiss
as would be

given to a
real mother,

the kiss given
had she been

my real
mother,

the kiss, the
tickle of lips on

her cheek, that
I did give

but never
in the right way,

the kind of
kiss that,

for her,
meant such

affection
as comes from

a natural
bond

that
a being

brought
to life within

another
would feel

for that
being.

A kiss not that
kiss, was all,

she felt, I ever
gave her, and

she deeply wanted,
needed, to feel

she was my
real mother.

She needed to
feel I was not

adopted, that I'd
come to life inside her,

that she gave
birth to me.

Of that immense
debt would

come
the kiss

she wanted, the kiss
she imagined my

birth mother
got from me,

whoever my birth
mother may

have been,
a Wisconsin

drug addict,
a college girl in

Arizona,
my real

mother, that
unknown woman

for whom
I was saving

my truest
affection.

Even in death I'm
no clearer

about what such
affection would

feel like,
or how

pressing my lips to
her cheek in some other

way would have
let me live,

such living as
that was,

brush of skin
against

skin, a tickle
like the flutter

of a butterfly
wing.

That's what
I kept from her,

that
secret kiss

learned at birth, that she
believed I

learned at
birth,

the kiss, right
to the end, I kept

keeping
from her.

XXII

Last night I dreamed I was inside
the *Bhagavad Gita.* A gate

shone before me. Beyond it,
the wonders of that

ancient epic. Passing
through, I stood

face to face
with the gods.

I had not yet
read the work.

I had only just, that
day, bought a copy.

If I'm being honest, this is
just the most recent

in a lifetime of
dreaming

about books,
the pages glowing,

the words seldom
ever legible in

the excitement of
revelation, pages

sometimes
blank but

always radiant,
composed of light.

XXIII

The tips of trees and grass
are touched by sun.

The rest is already the color of –
when, in 1940, on an abandoned

lunatic asylum, columns,
a stone staircase, like a bank

or a courthouse – what all
will be when night falls.

It's like a Mississippi
faerie palace that

disappears at twilight.
Already only the barest

corner is visible through
the trees. Below the cupola,

a bright ring of metal,
like a fence of fire atop

the six-sided dome.
That the place is visible

seems inadvertent.
The trees and tall grass

now zones of total black inside
the shadow of a looming.

That black rectangle
rising within white stone

at ground level, like a headstone
or an entrance to a crypt

in this photograph of
a madhouse, a door,

a portal through which
every soul passes

to win a body
and be here?

XXIV

If the result of the sky is a rose.
If the result a stone is the ocean.

      *

If the grave is a kind of gift,
and lassitude, of rapture.

      *

If a backwater town
strives to be a resort,

and melancholia
a form of fidelity.

      *

If coastal destruction
is a Renaissance chapel.

      *

If the thin mist is
a stream of rain.

*

If sunrise turns earth
into clouds of islands,

*

If boats are what sail
beneath the earth.

*

If the One is the shining
fruit of dividedness.

*

If Saturn leaves the zodiac.
If sleeping deepens grieving.

*

If the ditch lacks depth
though prisoners dig and dig.

*

If the Passion happens again.
If a pool shimmers with green light.

       *

If I dump red paint on a bed.
If flowers are vibratory meteors.

       *

If thoughts break white over rocks.
If those dogs are barking at a bird.

       *

If I might be whoever it was
took a hammer to *La Pietà*.

XXV

In the Vedas, regarding
the fire god, Agni, why

should he only grace the fields
of India, Mongolia, China, Malaysia?

Aren't there blinding
eruptions of dry grass

awaiting him elsewhere?
Amazing to see, even at night,

darkness pressing so
close to the flame.

The blackness of the field
runs up, and into, the brilliance,

as if the blackness is
what is flickering,

lashing into the
shimmering blaze.

And here the grass
is tall and thick, curls,

squiggles, a bounty of
tenacious growth, a jungle,

knee-level, with crisp
blue sky above,

a scarf of orange silk
pulled through the depth of

the grass, as if a beautiful and
enigmatic woman is

undressing, casting off
a slip while running

down to the sea. Along the mud
a tangle of branches is

red on one side, where
the world is burning,

where Agni walks around.
The other side, cool and black.

Night consoles the trees
regarding what

they're about to endure.
Eventually, Night says,

a white mist will cover a field.
The earth will seem purple.

The horizon will be
nothing but dust,

as if there is a shroud
around the planet.

Space will turn
to pale aqua . . .

*

At Jacob's Mound, a gully of fire
is roseate, erotic. The trees split.

Vs of flame streak the tender inner wood.
The sap is burning as it rises.

Near the cattle pens, black ground,
cooling night receding, crests of

burning grass are waves
reaching a beach.

Abruption of fire,
froth in a black swell,

as when, sinking in a war
movie, the conning tower of

a submarine full of heroes
drops away into black . . .

*

Long ago, in the old neighborhood,
kids had a task, tending flames

with rakes, burning gutters
of weekend leaves burning,

as well, in a huge empty oil drum,
the week's trash. In the snow,

drips of molten blue
dry cleaner's plastic,

detergent bottles, and
the deep blast of aerosol cans.

        *

Here and now, it looks like
in Chase County, Kansas

a spaceship has crashed.
The sun having set, the horizon

is bands of color. A layer of
soft white floats above the orange.

Night waits to pour down,
waits to drench what's

left of the world.
In any field, the edge

of a fire makes for
a second horizon.

No way to see beyond it.
On the plains of Plano,

Fire's a pit of luminous
smoke, smoke rising

into the night sky, reflecting
flames that can't be seen.

*

South of Emporia the night sky
is immense. The trees are only

starting, there, to burn.
It's early in the cataclysm.

They seem concerned to
keep a formal distance

from each other. Then
a sheen of fire falls on a field,

as if the sky itself has caught fire,
as if the sky were a fire

rising from the center
of a lake at night.

XXVI

Gethsemane

Vespers. Feast day, the Queen flies back.
(And, mother, this would be your birthday.)

Inside, monks in black and white
are about to start chanting.

And here is the grave of Father Louis,
Thomas Merton, one in a row of white crosses.

XXVII

Whatever the rituals,
this is where they

did them, where one
could crawl into dirt,

get buried with a bowl
upside down on

the head, the
cosmos painted

on the inside of the
bowl, a hole punched

in its center where
the coil that made the

bowl began, so
souls can fly free.

XXVIII

Rising over the ripples as
the lake pulls free of darkness,

in the mountains outside the city,
a meteor shower scratches the blackness.

A boy and girl are kissing.
But what rules you now

is a light beyond this moonlight,
is houses, planets, the angles

of relation, is spooky exactitude.
The heavenly influences

wash through each other.
But darkly, through them all,

with an effect so unlike
the glowing rings that

astonish schoolchildren,
the annihilating rays of Saturn.

XXIX

The cops said stop.
I guess I didn't. First

two, then six piled on.
I got some kicks in.

You should see the bruises
on my back, the rings

around my wrists!
No one, least of all me,

denies force was needed!
And there were, it seems,

sharp verbal exchanges.
(I'm not sure about

 the timeline.) I have,
I've been told,

 the adrenaline of
race car drivers who,

after a wreck, don't recall
the wall, the flames.

XXX

In this kind of hospital
we all get fake names.

Each arrest, a new name,
Nothing too pop culture.

Nothing too Bible sounding.
A few days here I ran into

a friend, a failed suicide
from last time, and failing,

obviously, yet again.
(The joke was his!)

We amused ourselves,
recalling names given

us on earlier visits,
and those we have now.

XXXI

Is this "of use?" Could this be
some key to the larger argument

always so close,
at last, to articulation,

close, without ever arriving,
not, in fact, one word,

one hint of a logic
trailing off,

a passing incandescence of evidence
making what you want

at last, defensible,
unprecedented,

the energy, the new life
that would surge

through you,
yes, like

a sudden love
that dishevels you?

Even just a rough sense
of what a defense,

even if only
intuited now, would

entail, a hint that
your desire,

indefensible as it is,
might no longer be so,

some irrefutable
intimation

that what you
wanted, what you

could be said to
cry out for,

could be defended, be claimed,
even if you were not,

would
never be,

whoever
history, narrowly

construed, would
judge

adequate, if
not exemplary,

having,
that is,

amid those years, that
cascade of miseries,

amid the meager intelligence,
the confusion of feelings,

sufficient
wherewithal,

(Whatever
wherewithal

could be credibly asserted,
in some last evaluation,

to be yours)
wherewithal

to advance, however
incoherently, your most

persistent and
indefensible

desire,
whatever

wherewithal might make
available to you,

if only for the moment
of your finding

the defense
and making it,

a sense of what all
this really is,

this life, this
path the sun cuts,

or what can be
seen of it, a flame

on the sheen
of a lake . . .

XXXII

Rose said: the church
is open all night. Do you

want to go and light
a candle there?

I said no, no bother,
no need for that.

*

But secretly, I wanted to go.
That night of all nights

I wanted to light a candle
in a bank of candles,

wanted to place a small flame
amid the multitudinous

flickers, like when, a child,
even then, I felt a bank

of candles in darkness
the one true altar.

*

Such a light would give
your ghost warmth.

Are you watching me,
wherever you are?

Rose said: your
mother was like

the peasants in Mexico,
especially when she pinned

a medal to your
sick bed, promising

God, should He
spare you, years from

that moment,
you'd take

as your Confirmation
name, the name of

the founder of monasteries,
the patron of a happy

death, who died
with his hands

raised to heaven,
the saint on the medal

snagged on the
cool white

plunge of your
fever sheets.

*

The church is just
around the corner,

Rose said, and
open all night.

*

And, as you may
remember, Rose said,

tomorrow would be, and is still,
you mother's birthday.

Not to mention, I said,
the Feast of the Ascension!

No, said Rose. What you
mean is The Feast of

the Assumption, the Holy
Day of Obligation declared the year

you were born,
1954, when the eternal

and the maternal
are shown to be

the same,
Rose said.

*

Rose said: Many medieval
books have been read, and read

by me. I know this night began long
before your birth, long

before your mother's birth.
Rose said: I've read books

older than medieval books,
books about the birth of the night

from which all came forth,
books about the precious tongue

of holy fire that descended,
a gift given to the world.

*

You remember, don't you,
how your mother lit candles for the dead?

I can never remember, I say to Rose,
not quite in reply, the day

or year she died, only that
it was early spring.

There were flowers in the trees in the park
like white, scented flames rising

from white candles.
I guess God lit them.

The flicker of fresh flowers
takes me back to the moment,

the moment I learned
that she was dying.

                    *

So I spoke, with Rose,
a woman not unmindful of

the mystical meanings of
her own name. I spoke

with Rose, in a bar in
San Francisco, near

a church, a church, open all night,
racks of candles, gleaming

gold, the candle stand,
the sweet wax scent

of flowers that
are flames,

where many candles
are already lit, many more

awaiting that touch of
purest fire, that ecstatic,

agonized burning
that a wick is . . .

XXXIII

When they scanned him,
his brain lit up, and

didn't. Parts no doctor
suspected were dark,

were dark. Much
about his life

then felt different.
We never got along,

my brother and me.
not as children,

not in adult life.
Now all I wanted

was to understand him,
to learn how we learn

about the world,
our sense data, our

thoughts, our belief
in who we are, fathom

how what comes
to be, comes to be.

When my brother
had a stroke, and a scan,

they saw his brain
was flipped around,

left and right,
reversed, little

lighting up
as it should.

When I saw that
for the first time

in my life I felt
I had a brother,

although all our lives
we were angry, unhappy, and

inexplicable to
each other.

We never got along.
Most of his adult

life my brother
sorted mail

at the post office.
He was, they said,

very good
at his job . . .

XXXIV

ghost of Juan Ramón Jiménez

That could only be Jiménez,
the singe in the silence,

the wind that routes
the shadow through the light.

Air empties out.
Wind is beginning.

Does it come
from the south?

Someone, ask the south.
Does it come from the west,

from the nest of
its gathering?

Some soul, go ask.
Nothing, at the moment,

stirs on the earth.
Walls creak. Vines tremble.

A surge, passing over,
rips through.

The tall thin trees, hundreds of
feet high rock in the light

in deep joy,
the joy which

when Jiménez lets me
see through his eyes,

reveals a crest of
perfection, running

through the world
washing agonies away.

But here below
only the most

tender of breezes,
like a compassionate hand

on the hot brow of
a woman giving birth,

immediate, yet
imperceptible.

Juan Ramón Jiménez might say
such breezes are sent

to bathe the world, to
liquify the light, to welcome

us into the air, air
full of warm

light on
a cold day.

He might say he sent this
gift from the north, from the east,

from wherever
paradise is

possible, sweeping
over the gleam of

a lake weeks
before spring,

a gust, a puff, white dust
blowing away

abandoned nests,
sparkling gnarls of thorns.

XXXV

winter solstice

The lengthening duration of daylight
can be proven, though you'd

rather deny it. Would
rather refuse to

admit what the ivy
climbing the bare trees

knows: brightness
is returning.

*

      In the gathering brilliance
      gloom intensifies.

      The brutal illumination
      of mid-June will defeat you.

      The delicious dark is fleeing.
      A life lived on a turning planet

      stirs, in you, no
      love of light's return.

*

(Conceived
in winter, born

in fall, those are
the seasons you find true.)

XXXVI

Just then, the moon
blew up, falling to the

ground as granules of
ice; the glaze

on the branches
what's left of what

the world knew
as moonlight.

In the morning,
patches of

lunar landfall
glow on a slope.

All alive now will
be known as the last

to ever see
the moon

in the sky, pale as
a snowflake

in the daylight,
enigmatic, mystical,

the moon now
blown apart, so

what is that light in
the dark, shining

on the side of
a darkened

and unfinished
foundation of a house,

starlight finally
touching an earth

unguarded
since the murder

of the moon
a faint coppery

orange washed over
with yellow

the shadowy
cinderblocks,

filling the
unlit pit.

XXXVII

Had some
flashing

                         chunk
not hit earth, set it

spinning, this
pen

would not be
in hand,

                this grief
not now fill

every thought   this cry
to see you

would not
exist,

long ago the sun
having

consumed
the last

longing in my
heart.

*

I'd be free.
I'd be nothing.

I'd be glittering
grit

scattered
throughout space,

indifferent to
the pull of

your purity,
warmth, light,

and your
perfection.

XXXVIII

How can you dream so deeply
and not be within the mind of a god?

How not aver you live behind
the closed eyelids of a god,

a god fallen asleep, who
sees all that will be?

How can you draw conscious
breath and not feel you are

the nostrils, throat, and
lungs of a living god?

How can you close your
own eyes, a second or two

midafternoon, and not know
you have entered heaven?

XXXIX

At twilight the metal of
the lake, though

dark,
is brighter

than the first of
the mountain's rising

into the mist
behind it.

Far away, a slice of
sky flows

molten,
while here,

blackness seeps
into

fir branches.
The glitter of the hotel

reaches an end.
On the rolling

lawn beyond the
boathouse

empty chairs
sink into shadow.

A few tall poles
in the water.

In the
morning,

no boats
are left.

XL

It's like stepping outside for
a moment from some

ongoing festivity,
freshly poured cup

in hand. Woods, clear moon
overhead, the scattering

of stars, sweet
woodsmoke scent.

It's like inside, the living
jabber and guffaw,

not yet noting
I'm not there.

It's like out on a porch
I'm sipping wine, watching

the moon move
into an open zone

between two trees
filling, now, with pale light.

XLI

As if ghosts had whispered
the universe has many

dimensions, and the rain
about to begin will

explain them. A puff
of hurricane passes

through the trees.
The air recants

its role as wind. In the
moment between heartbeats,

some invisible delight
brushes the skin.

Stillness brings
things to be.

No motion's free of it.
This dirt mound

will be an orchard.
The gleaming trails of

snails mark paths of
spiritual ascent.

This is as close as
any ever are to

the second life
of Lazarus.

The tree, slept
under, exploded.

None had ever seen
lightning strike.

The next day, one of
the boys wandered

into a whirling
mist of bees

and walked out
untouched.

CHAOTIC PENDULUM

THE ASCENSION OF NATHANAEL WEST

Enoch, you lifted me through the heavens
which were puffs of bright dust around a dump site.
The sky was shining through the blown-out backs of buildings
as if I were in a cab about to pass Marcus Garvey Park.
Why had I thought holy books nothing but porn,
tabloid shreds of black and white joy
found in the dirt behind a childhood barn?
Prophet, we entered a gate of tinfoil
and lightbulbs. You disappeared. An old man,
dignified, putrid, walked up to me while
I was poking through a heap of costume jewelry
laid out for sale on a street vendor's rug.
He claimed he would reconcile the world's religions,
but the clientele in his building has changed over the years.
He now lives among drug addicts and nutcases.

STRIKE FORCE

The balloon in mist, awash in a branch. Wet petals cling
to your face as you step to earth again. Spotlit monuments. A
castle under siege by exuberant police whom the friend, with
you in your flight, dubs "a Pentecostal strike force." Inside the
castle, fortress, besieged house or cult compound, are certain
people from your past. The scent of wet petals and the feeling of
buoyancy still flood your mind. They are a confusion you want
to remain within, sweetly preferable to the phantasms inside. The
breeze shakes wetness from the silver and black leaves, from the
entangled balloon.

MY LIFE IN THE THEATER

The next room I rented had a window.
It looked out on an airshaft, and into
a world-famous cancer ward.

Patients shambled by all hours.
Shiny devices got wheeled between beds.

I was a guard at the Met.
On break I smoked in the basement.
The ceiling was a grating in the
sidewalk and looked up

at the shadows of
beautiful women arriving
to revere art.

After that, I happened to live where
Lorca lived when he wrote *Poet in New York*.

I, too, was a poet in New York.

I'd see the blue above the street and say:
I, too, feel assassinated by the sky!

Fabulous things quickly occurred,
nights no excess was beyond me.

I ate like a horse, yet lost weight.

I read *White Buildings* and chanted:
"My memory I left in a ravine."

I fell in love with an actress,
Tanya Thermador, dazzling but cruel.

She'd read about radical theater.
It was up to us, she said, to destroy

the bourgeois divide between life and art.

Under her spell I stole lumber
from construction sites for a secret stage
in an abandoned slaughterhouse.

The whole radical theater troupe
was infatuated with her. She required
each to sleep with her, in turn,
men and women alike, while
rebuking each:

"Love is the least of the
suffering our art demands!"

As her father was a drill sergeant
and a drunk with chronic rage disorder
back home on a base in Oklahoma,
she had a powerful capacity to
get others to get things done.

Yet, the premier project,
the Strindberg marathon,
never happened.

We did, however, put on a night of
Brecht poems making great use of
buckets of stage blood
and Nazi paraphernalia.

Our Russian émigré director
had twenty minutes to leave Russia.
A diplomatic door swung open
and Lev ambled through,
dreaming of the revolutionary
theater group he'd create in New York.

He called the troupe *Theater in Action*,
but we soon became known, among
friends, as *Theater Inaction.*

The plan to commission
poets to write bold new works
for the stage went nowhere.

Our theatrical rendering of the then
topical Jeffrey McDonald story,
the *Fatal Vision* soldier who
murdered his family
then blamed hippies who,
he said, wrote on the walls
shocking insults in blood,
much in the manner of
the infamous Manson
murders, came to nothing.

All agreed Tanya
should play all the parts,
killer and victims alike.

We were delirious to see her
deliver some grand, vaunting,
searing speech, like out of Euripides,
shaking with rage,
her small frame blood
soaked and semi-naked.

II

Around the time
the hostages returned from Iran,
their tickertape parade cutting through midtown,

I saw Ensor's sketches for
Christ's Entry into Brussels in 1889

and dreamed Christ was entering Manhattan.
FDR Drive. Centurions stood watch.
Posters, banners, confetti, spangles.

I was on the film crew filming it.
I had a line: "Hail, King of the Jews!"

A jury looked on from an off-camera box.
Jesus could be seen dragging his cross
underneath an overpass.

Whirls of tickertape.

Notable actresses of the day
each in a white frock
impersonated

a different Roman goddess.
The scene required each to hold
a birth control pill or a diaphragm
up to the camera

before succumbing, each in
succession, to seizures of terror.

Could this be the seed of
an original, collectively written play?
But Lev had gone back to Moscow,

Though the troupe was jazzed to act out
the dream, improvise a crucifixion
on our slaughterhouse stage

Theater In Action dissolved.

Tanya took a day job
on the floor of the stock exchange
which she would often call
the true theater of cruelty.

Then one day at the height of a selling frenzy
she got sexually assaulted atop
a desk at Smith Barney.

The Ensor inspired historical pageant
seemed, then, less compelling.

Tanya was on dramaturgical fire!

She sketched out Foucault's *History of Sexuality*,
Vol. 1 as a series of comic vignettes.

The troupe, none more than I,
worked fiercely, non-stop, for months,

sometimes through the night,
on this new, never to be staged
farewell to our art.

WHAT SHE WROTE

Zeus and Hera were arguing again.
Sunlight was beginning to lighten the air.
The clean-up league picked trash from clumps.
Elizabeth Taylor wrapped a snake around her arm.
Jackie O window-shopped along Madison.
Agamemnon wanted the war to go on forever.
"Things were better when you were sick."
Then sang the songbird in the cage:

That's how it is on this bitch of an earth!

A car burned serenely on the off-ramp.
Kids rushed out of the park to watch it burn.
Some planets were yellow, some blue.
Nancy and Sluggo made a suicide pact.
Forsaking the love of a settler woman
an Indian flung himself from a high rock.
In ceremonial robes I heard cries of dread
otherwise lost in the rumbling of momentous effects.
Someone was pinned, indelicately branded.
The tableau featuring satyrs and
Amazons had been painted over in red.
A redemptive figure stepped forth.
Tanya wrote in toothpaste
on the kitchen wall:

That's how it is on this bitch of an earth!

The walls kept darkening.
Nearby buildings took on the
grey of an eternally raining sky.
A boy closed a book. A dragon
burst into flame and vanished.
In the Bible, Mary and Martha
were cursing Jesus. In the trees,
a shattered videotape chassis,
nest a gobbed tangle of tape.
What vast epic was bleaching
back into invisibility there?
One where the toppled king
hired as a clown by a butcher
hands out leaflets about meat.
Pluto prayed for Persephone to be gone.
Hippolytus fell and bled. Phaedra,
unprompted, drank the poison.
A treacherous twilight kept falling.
You'd yet to gaze into the silver pool,
the one at the cleft in the rock, had
yet to see the horror of what you
had become. Only then will the
sexiest young woman ever to play
Estragon in all Oklahoma write
in toothpaste on the kitchen wall:

That's how it is on this bitch of an earth!

Zeus and Hera, their dew freshened the flowers.
They were saying, "We're going to a party!"
But you said, "No. I'd rather bind these
sheeves in the dust, then sip cool water."
Smoke drained into the sky from the roof
of the hospital cafeteria across the street.

A cloud in the shape of a bus rose up.
Came then voices in a chorus around
the corpse of the fallen hero, the savior
of the city, the warrior-citizen Hector,
who would keep these women from
becoming slaves, concubines, and
servants to the wives of foreign generals.
Hector, whose dying words turned out to be:

That's how it is on this bitch of an earth!

The emperor fell into a funk. The
perversions performed, he ordered
man and wife hauled off and shot and
thrown in a pit with the rest, sensing
as he did, in a moment of rare reflection,
a new era of spiritual plagues was dawning.
Fits of self-torment and black moods
break out but in far-off places.

That's how it is on this bitch of an earth!

You were on the walkway of a huge dam
at night in the dead of winter in Vermont
taking measurements for next to nothing pay.
At the opening of the film Belle was singing:
"There must be more than this provincial life!"
You, too, wanted life to be light and jaunty
but were distracted from that ambition
by feelings of persecution and dread.
Agonized voices rose into your mouth
from beneath the playground dirt.

Asteroids with the names of gods
swept by the earth, then disappeared
into a pulsating and purple depth.
When you left the apartment, it was bright.
When you got off the crosstown bus
it was pouring. The breeze from the river
found its way into a dark apartment.
An after-flash of an agony filled
the space around a dying star. Long
hours, a lonely telescope, just to see dust
come into being, dust once a world
of breezes from a first sea, dust
once stones with holy names.

That's how it is on this bitch of an earth!

Diomedes was experiencing acute self-division.
Athena needed a topical antibiotic.
The blessed act seemed more and more
like a stabling, a bungled stabbing
on a rollicking subway. You thought
you were Hector. You were Helen.
Andromeda noted, "I'll get the
children, you get that, don't you?"
A wren bravely caroled in the dark:
"Those hateful things I said? Forget
about them. They were about me."
Heat deaths mounted. No one went out.
The asphyxiation was obvious now.
The train shot out into daylight.
You thought you were Helen. You
were Achilles. You were a monster
who destroys everyone around
him because he's so proud. Your

astral body was off somewhere.
In your despair you felt the planet
dwindling into one final, twirling toxin,
reclaiming its birth as a poisonous welter.
The days slid away, but at least you
were in touch with the great beginning
of the cosmic cycle. Leaving for Nepal
you ran into friends on the street.
You avoided looking anyone in the eye.
How is it on such a beautiful day, you asked,
it's still such a long crawl towards any light?
O wretched maiden, betrothed in an evil time.
The shopkeeper screamed at the street vendor,
kicking over his display of junk. You've
read nothing that matters to you since
that high school autumn: *The Dubliners*,
John of the Cross, Alan Watts, Euripides,
The Fall of America, and *Wisconsin Death Trip*.
Ambulances brighten the flow of traffic.
In the world of purity, other versions
of this scene were shot. In one you affirm
kinship with the flying weasels of Australia.
Your annihilation, you come to find out,
is like a line of credit opened in your
name but without you knowing
about it. Why bother. You're not
authorized to use it. *Hey look! Here are
some pictures of me in a parachute!*

That's how it is on this bitch of an earth!

You dream you are back living with Antigone
in a sublet overlooking a park notable for

shootings at night. The mythological
extravagance worked for day and night
in a deserted slaughterhouse turned
experimental theater never came about.
Not even that musical version of
Murderer, the Hope of Women,
the set meticulously imagined
as an expressionist daycare center.
Rain escorts a turbulence across the sky.
The evening is an elegy for organic life.
Amid dust particles, hydrogen clouds,
radio waves, and concussive nuclear
reactions, a last cell pulsed with life.
A satyr gets torn apart by bored nymphs.
A god flays the intransigent semi-mortal.
This was to be a belated love song for
an audacious actress, roommate, who once
smeared in glittering green toothpaste
across the kitchen wall one night:

That's how it is on this bitch of an earth!

You feel like you work for a moving company
but never get to put anything down. After
a cool night, the lingering heat returns.
There are cycles of rage without cycles of
renewal, lapses in pain without blossoms
of pleasure. The walls were charred.
You sat under a general's gold stature.
You wondered about a truer condition.
You were a child who says he knew
what existed before the Big Bang:
a gold dot the size of a quarter.

IN THIS MOVIE

In this movie, storm-blown fires swept the earth.
(It was a documentary about beekeeping
but with a clever, geo-political spin.)
In this movie, the action took place in a quarry.
In this movie, a convert to a cult scolded
her son for gloating, made him slap himself.
In this movie, intimacy led to outbursts of
bitterness and the belief passion was for animals.
In this movie, only those condemned to
eons of further incarnations were
foolish enough to procreate, though
the actress who said so was a scamp.
In this movie, rage met with deep affection.
The angles of a triangle didn't add up.
Your face was held between the hands of
a long-lost love, you were forgiven and kissed.
In this movie, communications were threats.
In this movie, snow fell in the mountains,
Arctic air poured down in late afternoon.
A moral dilemma had no resolution
then a tropical storm melted Antarctica.
In this movie, a bridegroom got injected
with alligator serum. He turned green
and scaly on his wedding night, and so
a murderer came to understand his body
was the vestment of his soul, and heard
a call from a god who was beyond
the heretofore furthermost god.
In this movie, dark hair was mesmerizing.
Men risked death to pick up Beauty's hairclip,
she a feisty slut performing miracles.
In this movie, trees whitened as we watched.

In this movie, children gleefully stole through
a hole in a fence and slid down the fairway on sleds.
In this movie, I was a Syrian diplomat and
a monomaniac, while you were
a microbiologist overly fond of shoes.
In this movie, it was all just security
measures and medical tests. The clouds
were motionless, but the trees trembled.
In this movie, high in the Alps, Milly Theale
looked down at the kingdoms of the earth.
In this movie, activists broke into the cathedral.
In this movie, languid adolescents jerked off
in a tent during a thunderstorm over
a beach as they look out at the lightening.
In this movie, my old teacher greeted me
on the sunlit steps. He was among the dead
and had spoken directly with Dante Alighieri.
In this movie, on the way to the courthouse
to marry a French showgirl the bricklayer
was assassinated by a jealous police chief.
In this movie, your mother lived on cheap wine.
In this movie, a delusional father struck his
dutiful son from all inheritance, while
a starving jazz drummer looked down an alley
and saw a full set of hand-hammered Turkish cymbals.

BEFORE THE THRONE
OF THE THIRD MILLENIUM

What distracted me

then, that I only feel this

now, & from what, now,

am I so distracted?

These incorporeal loves

where God lingers

at ruin's edge? Or that

woman askance in black,

her wake in the hotel pool

is all you see of her.

Primary colors fade

from the ferry. Water,

turquoise, amid Mexicans

at dawn, arms full of

Christmas gifts, but

saying the word God

twice, she could only

mean to be hostile.

The table's a mosaic.

The grapes are amethyst.

Eliminate or transfigure

structures of crumbling iron

pillars, tires in heaps, battery racks,

wooden slats. Make of

the biscuit warehouse

a munitions shed.

The body, burned. The wreath,

a ceremonial cusp of fire,

a loving explosive at the neck.

Boat, half emerged from light.

So, too, that green swath,

the material world.

CHAOTIC PENDULUM

Some of these serpents live in trees

and some are bred to have a color that

could never survive in the wild.

That exact anaconda was an extra,

had real screen time in the movie, *Anaconda*.

The funhouse had a chaotic pendulum.

It kept a crazy time, arms flapping

like those of a scarecrow in a high wind,

but you preferred the corridor of

Intergalactic Space, where you can

put your hand out and feel the

whirl of stars through your fingertips as

someone says: "I've been married eight times

but they say the ninth time is lucky."

      (So close, your face in sleep.

      I saw each emotion crossing it

as you shook your head.

I kept asking the same question,

thinking that you might

suddenly say yes.)

FRESH MANDALA INK

In a spring meadow, wandering off
the path, silver-haired man,

pink sweater. His daughter
finds him rapt in the center of

the wind that signs the name
of Creation over and over, too

fast to read, on the grass tips
which surge and flatten

like water in a tide pool
as the sea returns.

*

The breeze comes to an end
in a divine tangle of black dogs.

The sun smolders, then lights up the lake.
Sometimes, you say, I'm like

a mad queen around whose
arriving caravan naked natives

dance in welcome to the New
World where she believes she is in hell.

*

Then, once again, you're the kid
who found, on the side of the road,

a bag of chopped up Swedish porn,
hid it in his paper route shoulder sack,

then, on a deserted patch of lawn,
tried to fit the shreds back together,

confused by so much beauty,
till all those scraps blew away.

*

Gnosis comes to an end.
All books must go back to

the library, even if the
library no longer exists.

*

Heat lightning, flash of
the path that brought you here.

Are you at long last awakening,
or, has the spell's hold deepened?

*

Hardly enough light
to glimpse, through a mist

torn by pine trees,
the mandala tattoo

on the shoulder of
your momentary crush.

WATER PARK

The medical equipment was spread out

in the desert, thousands of IV bags

best stored, so the labels said,

between 50-70 degrees.

The pills had made the membrane

around my brain permeable,

but once that membrane is flushed

the pills won't work again.

The fields beneath the sheet of mist

are yellow green, with water in black pools.

The horizon keeps dropping back,

the sky keeps bending down.

You could say we were understaffed.

Clouds, low, scattered, bright.

The woman we sent to the

Registry of Graves was the only

one of us who could write.

(She had once been a schoolteacher.)

Later, I sat inside the drizzle of

an indoor fountain at a family friendly

waterpark resort sipping whiskey

passersby took to be coffee.

In my head a voice was singing

"Jesus don't want me for a sunbeam."

UNDER THE PRESSURE
OF RECENT DEVELOPMENTS

TROY

Long after Troy fell, the men still got caught up in melees down by the water. Behind what remained of the walls, music flourished, as did, despite the ravages, feasting. Romance revived, though few warriors were left fit enough to come courting. Wedding ceremonies evolved. Arbitration regarding exogamous mates became customary. If her blood kin did not show up, shouting abuse, the bride felt worthless. Decorative arts flourished, though icons of Trojan gods lost their glamor. After some time, the families of the men who died in the war seemed just sad, no longer tragic. Life in Troy became more and more like when you were a kid and, down the street, some other kid had a parent who got cancer and died. You didn't think about it all that long. You felt bad, but it was not hard to forget.

ARCHIVE

Middle of night, all asleep, the appraisers came. They broke open the archive. They took away the treasures. And so, all's gone elsewhere. Was already elsewhere if it, in fact, were ever here. If it seems here now, that's the proof it's elsewhere. Your hand would pass right through the treasure were you to try and touch it, or lift it, or steal it away, or protect it, whatever the treasure is, possibly nothing like a manuscript or artwork or letter or bit of clothing. Some would like you to believe the archive is intact, inviolable, despite rumors of disappearing treasures, hints of sales in Japan. Yet even those who believe all has been preserved cannot say for sure where the true archive now is, or how, if it is scattered about in several places, it can be said to exist as a single archive and not as a desecrated, pillaged ruin. What heightens anxiety about the archive is that no one knows what it holds. So much could be there, in the archive, were the archive there. Speculations among aficionados adhere to a plausible limit, though there is no accounting of contents that might restrain wonder. Those who sealed the archive, those to whom the keeping of the archive was entrusted, long ago, by the man whose life's work was the heart of the archive, many of them have also died, have died and also left no instruction as to how the archive should be managed, when, if ever, it should be unsealed, or sold, or if anywhere are clues about what is inside the archive, if anything is left. Lawyers lurk at the edge of the archive. If you imagine the archive as a golden box with elaborate carvings, also in gold, on every panel, and a roof like a lid, also gold, and if you then picture the golden box afloat on an ocean at midnight, the lawyers would be like swimming snakes twisting through the waves around the floating box.

UNDER THE PRESSURE
OF RECENT DEVELOPMENTS

I intended to talk about that, at some future point, that pressure, what it is, and so recent. I intended to talk about those developments, what made them what they were, were to me, that I felt them as pressure, pressure arising from the failure of the enterprise, that was one, then, what the victors intended, that was another. Caution had been urged, and silence, as per the developments, so recent. Who could be sure what was happening? No one knew what was happening. Experts were sent for, the most abject offered insights, forces, it seems, were at work, long before there were developments, what I might recognize as developments, from where I was. The pressure got to me. Had been, in fact, getting to me, I now realize. Developments were happening, affecting me. I was a part of them. But I denied they were happening, denied, under that pressure, what was said then, to whom, by whom, swayed as I was, amok with the implications. Then came gaps in the pressure. Sudden calm. As if all was alright. As if I were dreaming the developments, the pressure. The calm got to me. Had none of it ever happened? Was it all as it was? Could I walk around the block, and no one be there when I returned, the gloom gone, and the dreamlike distance from others, those spared recent developments, those not wracked by forces at work? Out of nowhere, a long calm, lifelong. Then, so abrupt, a development. Morning birds in the field, black and white, ravens, gulls, clawing mud for seed. I was troubled, just for a second. Developments receded but the pressure did not. What then was, is, unclear, though I was there, went out for a walk, under the pressure of what, then, was, no one knew what that was, among those there, the long vigil, developments unfolding, others called for, forces at work, swayed as I was. I thought my cry was apart from the pressure, pressure I felt, due to recent developments. All during this time feelings preoccupied me. Developments kept happening. No one could do anything. The developments brought the pressure, which was, as I have said, what my feelings were, but the pressure came from beyond the developments, which, after all, were, then, still quite recent.

II

It was out of the Bible, or some other old book. No one believed this was what that was. Gloom, long foretold. And yet they were recent, the developments, the pressure, also recent. No one there denied it. It had not been and now it was, a confusion I shared, having been there, feeling those feelings, unclear what was happening, when the developments would cease, which no one wanted. I was getting more and more unclear, under that pressure, swayed as I was, by those developments, by how I felt as I saw them unfold. And what they showed. My cry only a part of what they showed, the forces, the ones at work, long before developments were perceptible. Such was what I, then, might recognize, might assume to be such, from where I was, so long it took me to see it, see developments that were happening. Much was hopeless, under that pressure, feeling that, and the others there, feeling that. What said then, there, all brought there, for that, the pressure felt, forces at work more than my feelings, developments, unforeseen, though as I said, long foretold. I amend that. Developments seen such as can never be foretold. Questions made it clear: this was the unknown. The unknown was happening to us, there, happening to one of us, there, hence, developments, those calling us there. Was I dreaming them? What dream real as that was? How so? That which was so real was the unknown happening, under the pressure, as has been said, of recent developments. The pressure was what I felt. Was death, that pressure. Was death what I felt? Like I was in the Bible? Was it only death making itself known, the unknown still forever beyond us? Us then feeling those feelings? Us brought there for that, for what was said, then, developments, still so recent, seen as such, said to be as such, us swayed by what was, by what I then was, one slow to see what was happening. No one knew what was happening. No one fathomed the forces at work. No one could say, under that pressure, what could be said, about the gloom, the dreamlike distance from others, the long calm, lifelong, and then a development, abrupt, but long feared, my cry only a part of it.

THE DAY IS A SKULL

There are only your ears to hear
what's in there, forever,
and only your ears
and what's in there, to
be heard, locked in your
skull as you are, no
more than a murmur
among murmurs, among
many murmurs, ears
to hear, him who, etc.,
forever and only let him
who has ears, hear,
a syllable, in the skull,
among murmurs
as you are.

Sounding
only, not forever,
a word never to
be heard, heard by
you, so you feel,
today. Others may,
hear among murmurs,
a word, fathom it,
locked in as each is.
Day is a skull into
which night murmurs
no more than the word *no*.
Only your ears to hear
it, if it's there to be
heard, If you're
there to hear it,
gently beneath
other murmurs.

What can you do?
You're locked in your
skull, hearing *No*
day and night amid
murmurs without
words, or only now
and then the word, *no.*
Murmurs, silence,
the word *no*, silence,
then more murmuring.
Are you alive? *No.*
So then, you're dead? *No.*
Only your ears to hear,
now, *no*, only your lips
to open and close
around it, joyous
at times, then stern?

No, whispers night
into the skull of day.
No, that shofar, that
wind of extinction,
sounding a note.
No, that red streak
of twilight. *No,*
fiery slash of day.
No. Has the word
come to you (*no*)
at last? *No,* the
eternal word? *No.*
Are you locked in
your skull, lost there?
No. Only your ears
to hear? *No.* Has
eternity begun?

No. Is *no* the only
word ever heard,
where you are? *No.*

THREE MATERNAL WOUNDS

I

Two tourists are stepping down from a helicopter onto
a rooftop in New York City. His mother is telling a man she
will die soon. She's telling him he should not worry, telling him
he should not be so upset. Then she talks the way she always
did, about everyday things, about things she looked at, told the
thoughts she had while she looked at them, looked, for example,
at the wall of a building outside her apartment. Slowly, over
years, she had noticed, beneath the drab, sooty brick color, a
fresco faintly colored in, and outlines of icons, holy faces, there,
under a century of filth. Christ was there, a severe, Byzantine,
a gold glow beneath bricks the color of dried blood. It was the
Christ in the church of his childhood, the huge gold, blue, and
white mural behind the altar, holding the world in one hand, and
showing his wound in the other.

II

On a beach in front of the house he summered in all
through childhood, he found his mother's bones. They were like
any driftwood washing up on the jewel-like sand but wrapped
in tattered garbage bags. It was sad to see her so. He was afraid
to touch the bundled-up bones. He drew back from his poor
mother. He felt ashamed. He woke with the sound of toppling
waves still in his ears. He thought of her bones, how beautiful
they were, poking through tears in the black plastic. They were
like sun-bleached seashells. No one had ever told him human
bones were so beautiful.

III

"I am writing this journal not for myself or for my children, though I hope it will comfort and teach them when I'm no longer here, but because the Holy Ghost asked me to. Brought my hand to this page, this page to my hand, so loneliness would not make me bitter. I had begun to know how terribly God, too, feels when his children leave him. Feels even their thoughts of him leave him before they even know they will leave him. When I drove back from choir practice it was very overcast. There was a wall of fog on the road. Cars a few feet ahead were barely visible. The fog was as white as a shining cloud. I couldn't see where I was. The air opened. A slow procession cut through the sudden clarity: a hearse, its open windows bursting with flowers."

AN EVER-HASTENING RETROSPECT

As if, at the end of it all, not quite the deathbed, but during the last long retrospect, a voice were to tell you, and, given who you are, it would have to be, would almost certainly be, a woman's voice, a woman your age now but who will be younger than you then, speaking with absolute authority, expressing a judgment that seems the simple elucidation of a single fact, a woman who took in all you had written, had lived with your verses, knew them, then said: "There were many bright spots, lines in succession or richly scattered, a stanza here and there, lively juxtapositions, learnedness but not too showy, well-considered metaphors, significant subjects rendered with degrees of freshness, and I had hoped, that it would come, passion would arise in you, not necessarily for me, but a feeling out of nowhere. I had hoped the brightly polished parts you spent your life assembling, would tremble with the force of that passion and redeem all you had done. But that did not happen."

PICTURES OF THE BODY

from inside the body

samples of the body from

inside the body

estimate of days

from inside the body

estimate of the days

the number, quality of

the days left,

inside the body

seeing from inside

your body pictures of

the body from

inside

the body

yourself as more

than how beautiful

the lungs look,

as more than

the delight of air

pouring into the body

as more than

the braid of muscles

nerves, tendon, bones

the flowing inside veins

no angel knows them

no angel knows

how when the lungs

turn against the breather,

heaven is over

the paradise happening

with every breath,

is done.

Word's come.

You took the tests

you had it all explained.

Heaven is over.

It's hard to hear that.

ST. OBJECTIVITY

I could not credit the blood in me, how brilliant, as it
flowed down me and over me and soaked me. I could feel the
wounds, so many, dozens, wounds from a knife, an unseen knife,
striking me from behind me. I was doing dishes in darkness.
In the darkness I had been savaged with a knife, at the sink, by
an intimate, an intimate in a spectacular fury, closing in there
behind me, me amazed in that moment, amazed how clear I was
thinking, calmly, almost serenely, almost delighted there was so
much more blood within me than without the stabbing I could
have believed. In the cool of my wounds, I felt open to the night
air. I kept washing the dishes. I kept talking. Then I was alone,
talking to no one. Speech, then, was the greatest joy I'd ever
known. I kept feeling the warm water flowing over my hands,
kept feeling my blood pouring down my arms. My wounds, cool,
fresh. The air of heaven circulating through me. I was one with it,
one with the starlight above the sink, above the trees out the huge
window that looked out on and into a forest.

VITA NUOVA

SILVER JACKET

"Who, let me ask again, in the Religion department, knows how to look good? Not Constance. She bleaches her hair white. Gauri wears saris, but then a jean jacket. (How convincing is that?) Sheer charisma makes Ralph attractive, but also: his sweaters are beautiful, first-rate wool. Karen looks sharp, and never thinks about it, whereas Lydia looks hideous, and the tragedy is, she works at it. There's Moll, a skeleton in leather. Imagine being in perfect health, with a new lover, a waitress, some kid without a thought in her head, and to look like that, like you're in chemo, and it's not going well! (Her scarves are not the silk you or I would wear!) As for me, I just bought a silver jacket. I can almost wear it all by itself, no skirt, though sitting down in public can pose a risk."

AFTER OVID

When you think of how we slipped away, lean forward in your seat. When you think of when we tugged, each to the other: touch the medallion at your neck. When you think of how I kissed you: push your hair back behind your left ear. When the sensation of my lips pressing against yours and not falling away at the first flash of nervousness, but holding, pressing more firmly, as if to draw you even closer to me: go ahead, put your arm around your husband. However dense the crowd at this gala, I'll see the gesture. I'll know you're thinking of me, of me kissing you deeply enough to draw to my lips the deepest possible joy, the bliss that lay long-hidden in the marrow of who you had once been, long before we ever met, when some great unhappiness came over you.

MY THIRD VITA NUOVA

From the dark, hand at eyes, from

the catacombs, in your other hand, sunglasses, coming out, into
the sun, long ago, a purse, maybe a satchel, slung, short sleeve
shirt, dark blue, striped pants, maybe cut-offs, your long dancer's
legs stepping back into the glare, decades ago smiling, no doubt,
dark hair pulled back, ringlets spilling, a shadow over your
left shoulder, up from below, your delightful, thrilling, wiseass
mouth, some remark of yours, now lost.

Seen, as from ahead, beyond

our emerging, me trailing the whole time, through the earth, an
afternoon, following you, your face, face turning back, face as if
candlelit, face in profile, past long lockers of bones. So cold. Did
one of us say that? Comment on that? Did that cold come with
us, with me, up into day, cold of the catacombs, cold carried
inside me, a torch of cold, unfelt, the whole time since. Is that
where it comes from, what I feel, cold, in my fingers, pen to
paper, and the warmth, pen against paper, as if, were I to write
more about you, quickly scratch, word, paper, word, paper, word
after word, warmth would all come back, the warmth of you,
back even here, in this cold, this day, a lifetime later, where I have
no idea where you are?

Martyrs under glass, in a row, aghast,

astonished, shrunken, having lost. Old gods not gone, not yet
driven out. Outraged saints, they see who leads us, Catholic
boy and girl, in a Christened underworld. However chaste my
infatuation, it is Eros, a god distant and dangerous, yet guarding

us, sponsoring us. You were older, a whole year, at sixteen, an
eon, had, had had, boyfriends. You seemed both sensual and
calm. The holy bones envied me. I had life. I had your attention.

A stranger met on a journey, all

wild thoughts, and a beauty that, even now, defies mention,
resists residence in words. Who, in your presence, did not feel
joy? A Sufi would know you. You were not "out of my league,"
you were a higher order of being. We were from different
ontological realms, different cities, had never met until this
trip, this extravagance planned by a parish priest and a local
clothing salesman who loved opera, show tunes, wine, who
sang as we drove through the Alps. You and I had never been
abroad. Everything astonished us: the lake at Lucerne, the
castles, vineyards, the legends of Petrarch. Even there, where the
sonnets were written, did I even allow myself, in the purity of my
surrender, to consider what it would be like, for, if not me then
my purified, transfigured double, to kiss you, be kissed by you?

Did we, at the steep turns, the jolt of

snow, see, did Love allow us, me, to see what they saw, what and
as, the Fedeli d'Amore, what they would have, looking at you, an
afternoon's cobblestone street, a shop, our charade, some spoof,
ruined by an entry bell. What they saw, I saw, not knowing what
I saw, would see, know, back home, the depth and dark of no
Alps, no Italy, only words, mine, witty ones sent to you, others
held back, kept, feeling, then, lost and dead, your gift to me,
unknown, as such, until later, when bitterness becomes a blessing,
places and words, rungs of a ladder, rung after rung, earth to
heaven, a radiance of words, perfection of the already felt, the
first felt, with you, amid all we saw. Though now I meander.

298

Details distract me. A memory: you, at the door, stopped, barred. The guard said: your skirt is too short! Not even a priest could get you into the cathedral.

Saint Mark's square, crossed, sunlit drizzle, and

from a café table, men saw the shimmer of air around you. They finished their espressos, they drowned themselves in a canal. In your passing by they had seen all that the world had kept from them. We were Love's witless messengers, knocking around for a free hour, admittedly the last hour in our epoch, the last before that historic hijacking, before nations were shaken, airliners rerouted, emptied, exploded in the desert. Stunned passengers deplaned in our stead, the week of our return, the world berserk with justice, the Holy Land ringing in the end time, that vacation in the last days of some fading order, around the time a zealot took a hammer to *La Pietà*. For some, it was the end of the West. For me, it was excitement.

All that old treasure, all Europe, came to me

through you, feelings for you, through talking to you, in earshot, all too often, of your chaperone, your aunt, a few days, even she seemed stoned, we all were, paradise of new places, with each step, afloat, none so much as Maury, the luncheonette owner's son, my aspiring rival, expertly fended, who found a truer devotion, anyway, on the streets (you and I wryly hit up for loans). All over the Old World, Maury scored hash. For Father Stu, the buzz of the secular. Doubt found him. (He left the order – did you hear?) A new truth touched him: small joys transform us.

Who could go back to the life that was, that went on,

back to those lesser canals, to Lowell, those reflections, the mills
on the water, so desolate, where the echo of your step did not
chime the cobblestones, where you never stepped. We'd seen
galleries and gondolas, those tableaux for the grand fables of the
modern erotic, they should have stayed with me more. But really,
the boats, the glory rising out of the water, domes of the Doge,
were transcendent only because they affected you. Venice is where
I was with you, where the god of passion once visited mortals,
exalted, tragic, where lovers ruled all thought, where, ages later,
a low-budget church tour of Europe, two high school kids see
the sights, two kids from two mill towns in New England, at
least for me, an epic romance (did you sense it?), a fable in which
birth placed us, and fate let us live, where a god kept guiding
me, to you, to a seat in a rental van, beside you, flashing on the
windshield, the history of the world, a priest at the wheel. The
salesman, the master of window displays, dazzles us with song,
the hash smoker clings to the last sweet hit of the night, deep in
the meander of his dream. And the youth counselor, Doug, both
upbeat and grim, lived with his mom, worked at an upscale men's
clothing store, he chaperoned teen dances, led retreats, he said he
was, at this point, more Buddhist than Catholic, my roommate,
we sat up talking at night, about love, suicide, homosexuality.
(He tried the third, thought about the second. Or was it the other
way around?) When all was over, was again pure nothing, the
week before boarding school, I hung around the store, dreamed
news of you might find its way to me from the Manchester
outlet, where your aunt sold shoes. I prayed some gossip could
find me, even here, even in Lowell, the anti-Venice, lesser canals,
deep, no doubt, in Whistler's memory when he etched Venice,
his lines so finely bitten into the metal. No one could believe how
much ink his metal could hold. No one could believe the glow of
those waters, the exactly rendered arches, the moodiness of it, the
"dry point lines, the luminous shadow of a palace doorway now

occupied by a chair maker," the "admirable manipulations of the acids." Venice, across a lagoon, all water, light, trembling, mast shadows, adrift in air, a hundred years before we set foot.

Like an old box, a letter in it, or the gap in

a gasp, pictures thought lost, now your voice, in the mind a moment, a micro-sensation, a last vibration, still there, to call me, steer me, to some small thing you notice, some last dividend, now, of your delight, the last of delight your touch on the arm, decades back, in the mind, now. You saw, wanted me to, what, magnificence, silliness, a vista or scene, then, an illusion, now, a prank, now, incompletely played, not consummately accomplished, until I remember some small thing. What patience, planning so brilliant a goof, years ago, a surge across time, a wave, a pulse lost to thought, decades, a wave of what, nothing, a wave through the mind, sent then, arriving now, from you, girl on a lark with an aunt, girl under the eye of a priest, to me, now, so that, now as then, I'm waiting, now as then, in the lobby, new morning in the Old World, some pensione, at the foot of the stair, thinking of you, long stair, waiting for you, once again, Europe means nothing, only what you will wear today, and your hair, how it will fall.

Canal, shutters, spill of light, quiet,

a shadowy room, a rare moment, on that pale replica of upper-class practice, the grand tour, now so democratized, that initiation, so diminished, that odd interlude between start and end of day, between your sleepy amble to the table in the morning and you, gone off with your aunt at night, in Europe, and I'm without you, in a room, alone. Dim light. Lap of legendary water. Was I even there? Was there any moment not at your side, chatting with you, taking cues from your irritation at my talk, early in the trip, Old World treasures ahead, you, pausing, considering, doubting. Was I worth the effort? A test. You said: "Why do you keep trying to use big words?" (Europe pulls back. Were we not to be the two? Would we be only ghosts in a catacomb? Europe panics. As do I. Europe knows Europe is nothing without you.) Then, more mortifying, more liberating, more precisely to the point, you say: "You don't seem to know what all your words mean." (Reader, taste my death. Feel the sear of my new life.) After that rebuke, that oracle, that barb, I had no choice. I spoke in a new way. From that moment, the only words, in my mind, on my lips, were what kept you, amused, engaged, earnest, and near, were what kept you choosing, each brilliant morning, to sit beside me on the long rides through Germany, Austria, Switzerland, and finally, Italy. Only through you would I see all the artworks, the legendary places. Philosophy was lost to me. I had traded truth for desire.

How long, an interminable time, you

dropping into dark, me entreating, you, now, unspeakably far, me desisting only for further inquisitions. On today's checklist: did I ever see you, your hair utterly down? Was your hair ever not pulled back, never more fully than in the comic knot you whipped up with one hand, so quick I could never catch it, adept as you were in the comic arts, made virtuosic, you conceded, by years of abiding the nuns, as you enter the prim swirl of your persona, the secretary, Betty. What other selves hide in you? How many do I miss, distracted in my adoration of the one I happen to know as Janet? Suddenly, at the picnic, on the mountainside, on a road through a valley, on church steps, where a moment before, you spoke of Dostoyevsky or Kafka, Betty is with us, saying impertinent things. What aunt can curtail "you," report back on "you," though she is so enjoying herself, she clearly doesn't care. After all, "you" mouth no outrage, but an out-of-the-blue worldly wise Betty. None got the best of Betty. No one summons her or compels her to appear. Only when a question is adequately overwhelming, the group lost enough, she might step into you and speak, or sing: as the van shoots down a mountain road, a risqué duet with Tom, the driver of the moment. Then Tom turns quiet. Betty vanishes. A new country enfolds before us. He's spent years, he says, drinking the wine of these hills. I know the taste of this place. I've sipped it from an ocean away, while looking at the labels, at pictures of vineyards, vineyards like these, now all around us.

The man at the wheel begins

an offhand hymn, to wine, to harvest, to vintage and year, he talks until he is, he says, dry as dust. We are dry as dust, listening to him, we find we are dry as dust, we're in a desert and dry as dust, we call out from the back of the van, we are dry, dry as dust, by the time a tavern appears no thought is possible but of wine. (Where is he, now, our sudden guide, or any of the others, Doug, or Father Stu, or Aunt Pat, or stoned-out Maury, where are they? What faraway life holds you? The Web turns up a multitude of Janets. None are you. Perhaps you're no longer here. Perhaps, like me, you're not yet alive.) Midafternoon. The tavern's all ours. Tom scans the wine list. There's no one in the world I'd rather drink with, now or ever, than all of you, he says.

MY SEVENTH VITA NUOVA

Not yet total dark

could he turn off the lights, she wants, red parka, band of white
down the arms, designs in black and blue thread within the
white, to tell him in the dark of the night, in total dark, in his
room, why they can't go out. In a chair, in the dark, she's talking.
The reasons are abstract. He, listening, kneeling before her, his
hands rest either side of her hips, his forehead touching her
knees. She, needing, she says, total dark, lights off, before she can
say, done, done, done with love, done, done, done. Face lifting in
the dark. All to be over before it started. Done, done, done. Faint
light, enough to kiss by, the talk having stopped.

What dark film art

left them, later, in snow, walking, a bluish glow to earth and
air, first light fills the sky, she was droll, confiding, en route to
her room, they're both serene, as if the intimacy had already
happened, transpired more truly in their talk. That they might
then go to bed, excite each other, lie quietly, seemed an after-
thought, all the while talking still more, about, what else ever,
but writing. The sex was also a prelude, of years to follow, in bed
and elsewhere, talking about writing, beginning this night, she in
silky purple, pulling out a notebook, a beautiful tale, a princess, a
crescent around her neck, grows sad, lightly cuts her wrist with it
as the moon rises. Later that night, his brilliant new love, reciting
from memory, "Westron wind, when will thou blow? The small
rain down can rain . . ."

To be the scholar she would be

much to know, Dante, Chaucer, The Pearl Poet, the Middle
Ages, all happening now, right in that room, in her, compass
points of lost worlds gathering around her, shreds of obliterated
compendiums, letters from convents, whatever light survived
the dark, classical languages in decay, Arabic science, plodding
French histories, heresies, love cults, conquests, banishments, the
expostulations of alchemists, the tracts of esoteric Imams, Saint
Teresa, the mansions of heaven, Saint Bernard, the soul's nuptials,
all and more called forth from the fringes of oblivion by her
study, by her devotion, already years along, her Medieval fever. In
the blue window light of the snow-crusted world near dawn, she
was suited, she said, deeply suited, to years, years, as if in secret,
years of preparation, she said, was saying, interrupted, then,
by the return of passion, strokes, kisses, delicate envelopments,
gasps, smiles, and sweet words.

A bus slows to a stop. All step out.

There is no station, in fact, no roads. The ground is red clay
brushed by blowing yellow sand. The sky is a rebounding white
glare. The two are apart, at far ends of the entourage. She is
smartly dressed, yet clearly ready for intense desert heat. He sees
her; she does not see him. He holds back. Their love did not end
well. Her magnificently caustic tongue could still cut him to
shreds. A second bus pulls up. No one is on it except the driver.
All of them on the trip are heading deeper into the heat. This
desert is only the first desert, nowhere near as overwhelming, so
he guesses, as what awaits each traveler, that second, solitary, and
absolute desert.

Kissing her was a delicious smoke,

breathing in, she, breathing out, cigarette between her fingers, – dangerous, the touch of that torch – yet sweetening the air while they kissed, while she held the intoxicant within her, kept it, kept it from him for a bit, holding the smoke, drawing the best of the drug of it into her blood, then breathing a fraction of her bliss into him. Through her, he drew in the buzz. Through her kisses, he craved tobacco, craved whispering blue smoke, craved her delicious wit, amid the slow dissipation of visible breath, the thin, sweet trails, he took from her, breathed out throughout the day, her ethereal taste in his mouth, a daze deeper than pot, drawn from darker leaves. Decades later he still tastes it, that new world narcotic, he can taste her, her dizzying kisses amid her scarves of smoke, her medallions of smoke, her dissolving adornments of smoke.

A painter disguised as a priest

hides a knife behind a large gold crucifix. He shouts: "Death to superstition!" He lunged at the Pope who, it would be revealed later, after the pontiff's death in 1978, found the failed assault on his life, during his arrival in Manila, "blissful." The painter, a self-proclaimed Surrealist, was arrested, but received a light sentence. It seems he ultimately confirmed the claim made by Imelda Marcos that her husband, the President, had single-handedly saved the Pope's life. The President had disabled the painter, or so it was told, with an expertly placed karate chop. This account momentarily revived the popularity of Ferdinand Marcos in this Catholic country. Yet due to widespread unrest and uprisings Marcos would soon declare martial law. This occurred in history, and in a short story written for a college class in Marxism and Literature. As a critique of bourgeois notions of authorship, it was decided by the collective that the story would be a collaboration

between two class members. He, an avowed Surrealist, was to
write two interior dream monologues, first for the painter, and
second the pontiff. These were to be read simultaneously at the
exact moment of the assault. His partner, an avowed Maoist,
gave an account of the event in a revolutionary style shaped by
dialectical materialism, but suitable to be read by the guerrillas in
the hills around the city, a style which, also, captured the rogue
violence of the hukbalahaps, who were believed by the class to be
capable of a certain anarchic sadism.

Only in the afterlife of now

did he see the truth of what she'd shown him that day, in an
obscure stack: a compendium of all the albas in the world. It was
an indispensable gift, though he only looked through it once,
and could never find it again, where he first saw this simple
poetic form, he would devote his life to writing over and over,
whatever the ostensible subject. Could she really have been so
precocious (yes, she could) as to say to him that all he would ever
need to know about poetry were these few essential elements: the
sun rising, the lovers flying, as the watchman makes his round?
Further, could she really have hinted at a secret meaning of the
rising fire, of the ecstasies in darkness, the higher truth of an
illicit touch, of the eternity of death the watchman could bring
upon them, from which only a friend, a friend of love, could
save them, warning them of the coming light, perhaps appearing
in the form of a bird. Could she have been candid enough (yes,
she could) to note the desolation of their separation after such
a night, after the blackness in the cup of night, the redness in
the cup of dawn; was it impossible that she imparted this, (not,
it was not) the gist of this, perhaps in the alchemy of their own
dawn, between kisses, in the tincture of a breathless embrace?
Remembering, then, her pale skin, her skin of moonlight, the
sharp, arched brow, her queenly profile, her posture sitting up in

bed, straightened back, as if hearing pleas or dispensing blessings. As if she knew things, could see things, say things, like no one he had ever known. Could she see her hurt at his betrayal as, a few years later, she became the wife sleeping in the town below, less the companion in passion than the betrayed. Could she foresee her anger at him, her tears at the wreck of their love, while he met a dark and wild witch in the woods at night? Did all of this, or none of this, lead her to tell him about his fate, the alba, the key to Romance in its most encompassing, world-creating sense, or was it a prophecy meant for her, that he'd leave her tender bower for a catastrophic love?

Above the bed where the sex is so

quiet, a postcard from the Cloisters, pinned on cloth. As a schoolgirl she'd go see the famous tapestries, the hunt and the death and the rebirth of the unicorn, that magical animal, dipping its horn in the waters, purifying them, so other animals could drink. Tapestry after tapestry, the world burst forth in pomegranates, hawthorn, oranges, pears, each plant vividly stitched and dyed. The cloth hung up on her thin dormitory wall was not bluish-green and grey but red, almost violet, the color of transcendental suffering. Brutally killed by dogs and spears, a living unicorn rests beneath a tree. It may also be, she says, whispering, and provocative, that the unicorn was not slain and reborn, but tamed by the touch of a lady.

Years later lines she read aloud in that bed

are with him night and day, in the dark, in the light, in the flame of the sun, in the cold of starless black, lines of the alba, an alba by Samuel Beckett, the death ahead of death, the blank sheet of the page yet to be written upon, crumpled, blowing down a dirty

Dublin street. But rereading, no body found on a street, in a sheet, bulk dead, though he will always imagine that, nowhere in the poem but that is what he sees, himself dead, saw as she read and sees now, her long vanished, to where in the world, don't know, though still her voice with the promise of the first lines still rings in his mind, her, in that bed, reciting:

before morning you shall be here
and Dante and the Logos and all the strata and mysteries

PASSING CLARITIES

BIRTHDAY CARDS

Each next is an
Ellis Isle. We arrive fleeing
the Cossacks of now.

A naked foot pressed my arm
to the sheet in a motel bed
at Deception Pass.

After the rain, the road
is the shade of fresh clay
on an art class table.

Tobacco leaves, hung on a rack.
Resin drenches the end
meant for burning.

In a dream the other
night, the alarm was off.
The vault, unlocked.

Executives in handcuffs,
a suicide in a far-off office
park in Oklahoma.

But should the stitching
be hidden when the thread
is so beautiful?

The nuzzle is not polite.
The kiss below the ear, startling.
(Beneath a green awning, trembling.)

Stray Lenten ash blows
in your eye. Tilt your head back.
Gaze into the water as it pours over you.

Awake, now, much has
not happened yet. The late
sun has not yet dried the dew.

Over the meadow, hawk shadow,
here trees looped with ivy loom
and streams roll pale stones.

Who visits me
in this wait for the last of the light
to strike the water?

On the road to the beach –
hand-painted Bible citations
nailed to trees fly by.

The pleasure fades. Bones
in your face ache. Desire fills
a bruised vein inside your skull.

Jaunt in the roaring fog,
under invisible planes, at
the edge of a field, lost.

A policeman points down
from the train trestle: *Right there.*
I found them right there.

Hydrofoils in twilight . . .
The road stops. Slope of mud
where houses slid into the water.

You pray to all the gods
of annihilation, *Let a new lie*
fill the hollows of my joy.

A cave erupts in a sky
shadowed by the late sun,
rayed in layers behind the peak.

When light lessens
the flowers grow more
colorful to our eyes.

PASSING CLARITIES

I

Inside the shoebox was a small branch and
each offshoot held a string of glass
beads like silver rainwater, and on
each bead a letter, the whole alphabet
in black, on glittering spheres,
branch more a sprig, a gift
left at the door by a woman,
black hair, black eyes that were
once described, to you, as haunted.
In fact, you hear the hesitant
allure of her voice as you read
the carefully typed instructions
that concern how you are
meant to gaze upon the letters,
the luminous fruit on the branch of
language that she has given you,
has made for you, has made
only for you to study, in
preparation for the opening of
the second box, so dazzling
in its intricate design that
you put it down, you are
not ready to proceed,
even among such simple
things as you have yet to learn,
the language she is giving you,
you have been stopped
at love's gateway, can only
recall that the cardboard squares
that ring the inner wall of

the second box have had
the square of film removed,
replaced with bright squares
of copper creating
her vision of the inward
heaven of the retina, the
sensation, so unexpected
in a shoebox, of torchlight
flickering on some ancient
trove as you open it, and find
yourself on a bus rolling
through the pre-dawn black.
The boats look magical in long
rows of the low-lit pier.

II

If only high-rises lined the street
on both sides they could feel
they lived in a tunnel.

She seemed then to turn to him,
however dead both were, and ask:

"After our breakup, did someone
else have our remaining joys,
then return what we were,
like a rental car, on empty?"

They were drifting away from life
as clouds from which their souls peered down
into our world like airplane passengers
looking down at the Bahamas.

There, gold and red fish in turquoise depths
mull around castles of white coral
like tattoos tucked in
scandalous places

showing couples kissing atop the rocks
before skiing down the mountain
in whirls of carefree snow.

More and more it was like
in Fra Angelico,

an ascending spiral:
figures entering heaven.

They were delighted to be
again, in their own bodies on a day

when the air will be gold.

III

Kicked out of JTS for

smoking pot.

*

For hanging with Rastas, reggae
cranked loud, talking Torah, stoned.

*

And so, I wound up in the wilderness of

a vast meat conglomerate,

a pig farmer in the south, insolvent,
on the mouth of a river, amid
the squeals and shit,
where the water table
does not permit pig burial?

(Dig a grave, it's all water.)

The dead are dumped in a bin.

*

After such dreams
I was no longer quite

Hiram, an Alabama mason

named for the guy
who built the first or

second temple,
maybe the third.

       (Or, was it
       the guy who tore
       them all down?)

*

I was afloat on flowers,
drifting on a singe of orange,
a scrape of pale yellow.

Last night, waking in a basement,
a broken pipe drenched the clutter.

*

I had not yet intimated
my final passion.
Her name, Joy Trial.

*

The trees were beyond
dismay. They were scraped
down to pink, white, violet.

Their blossoms pain them, and
new leaves tear them apart.

*

(I will never be what the age praises.)

*

I was lost, then, in her dark,
elegant thoughts, wild
gestures hypnotic as ever,
her complicated novels
and art devotions,
her epic and ongoing
psychoanalysis.
The shimmering silk of
her dress was intensified
by the pace she loved to walk at,
New York itself never
fast enough for her . . .

*

My hope had been to marry
a painter, who, when
I died, would fill a wall
with glowing,
moonlit disks
amid crumpled
colors, like suns
rising on some
imponderably
far planet.

THE MINISTRY OF CHRISTIAN CLOWNS

I'm a clown for Christ.
At work, everyone knows,
even my boss. He didn't
like it at first but now
he's cool with it.

Everyone loves to
exclaim, "What a clown!
You're such a clown."

When I walk into my job
a guy always yells from
the top of the stairs:
"Hey you clown!

Hey there, you
fucking worthless
Christian clown!"

*

I always carry
two sheets of paper
with writing on each,
so I can read out
whatever the
occasion calls for.
One sheet says:
"All of Creation
was made for you."

The other says:
"I am dust and ash."

*

Recently I qualified to perform
at churches, certain hospitals,
and at Sunday schools.
Amid the juggling, jokes
and making animals
out of balloons,
I might tell a story.

*

A good man and a bad man
ride an elevator to heaven.
The good man has a passport.
(I hold up some paper.)
The bad man does not.
The good man wants to
share, and tears off a piece
of his passport, like this,
and gives it to the bad man.
But the bad man wants
more and more of the
passport to heaven.
The good man takes pity,
tearing off more and more
as the elevator rises.
(I demonstrate.)

*

When the door of the
celestial elevator opens
in a bright blast, Saint Peter
asks the good man: "Why
should I let you in?"
The good man unfolds
what's left of the paper
that is the passport.
Incredibly, it makes
a cross! The saint says,
"Welcome to heaven!"
The saint asks the same of
the bad man, and the
bad man says: "Oh,
I had a rough trip. Mine
got messed up. In fact,
it's just a handful of scraps."
Saint Peter says: "Don't worry.
See, it's still good. Look!
It tells me right where
you're going!" Then
Saint Peter (that's me)
lays out the strips of paper.
They spell out HELL . . .

*

I've added to the show
my own kind of Bible stories.
For example, I don't talk

about Jonah. I talk about
the whale. Jonah knew
about God and was
amazed not to die.
But in my version,
I tell how the whale felt,
giving birth to a higher
form of life out of its own mouth!
After a miracle like that, how
could any fish go back
to life as it was? So
I make up adventures.
I imagine death so
intensely that who
I am washes away.

*

It's like the way
the body of the crucified
is always on the mind of
those women mystics
of the Middle Ages.
Like them, I pray:
"Grant me this grace:
That since Christ was
crucified on the wood of
the cross, on top of a hill,
nail me up in a gully,
on an old rotting tree.

Grant me a slower,
more horrible death.
Hear me, Lord, and
grant me a death
vile enough to
match my desire . . ."

NOT THOREAU

for Geoffrey O'Brien

A man in 19th century
America lived alone in
the woods in a small cabin.
This man, who lived in
the woods, was not
Thoreau, though in
the end, he also died.

The youngest son of
a renowned murderer and
millionaire, this man,
who went to the woods
also, in his way, to
live deliberately, this
man not Thoreau, and
slit half his throat.

Halfway through slitting
his throat, this man
changed his mind.
He took his half-slit throat
to a neighbor at the wood's edge.
The neighbors bandaged
up the throat. The man
returned that night
to the woods, to the cabin
he had built by hand
where he, like Thoreau,
lived deliberately,
though Thoreau did
not slash his own throat.

Having cut half his throat,
having then changed his
mind, having got bandaged,
returned to his cabin,
his very own Walden,
changed his mind again
and completed the slashing.

Those extra few hours,
between the beginning
and the conclusion of
the slashing of his throat,
what did they mean to him?

PASSING CLARITIES

To sketch progress

on graph paper that is as pale

as a ghost crab shell on the tidal flats,

now that a part of the line is

longer than the whole.

Now that ¾ is greater that 4 ½.

Now that, in our stillness,

we have travelled
"a negative distance."

The air is sweet today.

A drumbeat floats over the hill.

What body do I wake within?

Last night was delightful.

My eyesight seemed enhanced,
almost digitalized: the details

in the distance of the dream were
as clear as what was up close.

The weed has a red flower.
Some of the petals are darker.

In the illusion of shadowy
depth, roses float in early sun.

The air seems bluish grey.

The residue of a mist
was reflecting the leaves.

I was free of horror and fear.

These days no one lies face down
on summer grass, absorbed in
a cosmos of pale tangles.

The masts are floodlit.

The burnished wood of the cabin
reflects the light broken up on the water.

A new yacht appears at the dock.

Inside, a woman in a red dress

slowly lights a candelabra.

In the morning the air is
like silk, but the yacht is gone . . .

L pulled pins from her red hair.
The flames fall down

around her neck, spill
against her cheek.

She had just set the whisky down,
eight glasses, four in each hand,

held from above as if
on strings from her fingers.

A magical act, the glasses themselves
two flowers of fire, floating

down, her hands above them,
free of them, blessing
their descent to the table.

Elsewise we are skeletons

holding empty bowls out to the air.

It's quiet here. No one can help me.

I was with you in a dream.

You pressed your hand to my face.

All the branches in the trees
are lifting in a wind ripping
away parts of the planet.

Or is that just a thrill pulsing through you,
sweeping your limbs, setting various
organs to trembling?

Unfold out of the folds of the storm
of the cold comes the divine heat . . .

That's when I fell in love

with you, Tanya Thermidor.

Your arguments about the immediate
collapse of the moral order

struck me as compelling.

Only bloodshed can cleanse
our ethics, you would say.

Then later, weeping,
you would add:

*I'm so tired I can
hardly lift my hand.*

NACHIKETA

The chant wins protection from the three realms of trouble. Then the infant is adorned with baubles, rings, bracelets, and a gold chain. As if he were ready to sip, a leaf-shaped cup is brought to his lips. The mother is relaxed, beautiful, in robes of deep blue, gold, and green, with a slash of red pigment on her forehead. For guests unfamiliar with Sanskrit, the son's name is explained. In a legend a boy sees his father giving gifts to death. The father never slays the good cattle, however, only the sick or injured or old. The son questions the logic of such a gift. The father gets angry. The father says maybe you should be given to death instead! The son says yes, I will go to the land of Death and speak to Death directly. The boy goes down to hell. Death is not there. Death is out in the world gathering souls. The boy waits. The boy is a Brahmin. It is rude to keep a Brahmin waiting. When Death returns, Death apologizes, and gives the boy three wishes. First, the boy asks to make peace with his father. Second, the boy asks to learn the fire ritual. These requests can be granted. However, the third wish cannot. The boy has asked to know the meaning of life and death, but not even Death knows the answer.

On a bed of unhusked grain poured on a red cloth with swirls of gold running through it, the name of the obedient, curious boy, Nachiketa, takes shape amid the letters appearing at the end of the fingertips of an Iranian woman in red silk. The mother whispers the name in the child's ear. This is the first time the boy has heard his own name. He's set down on the bed of grain. He's nestled amid the letters. He feels the force of names swirling about him, the names of ancestors, heroes, gods, demons. He feels the force of names not yet bestowed on those not yet born. He hears them, names too sacred to say, he hears them. He lies quiet. He makes sounds. One day the sounds he makes will be names, perhaps one will be the name of his true love. At a table in the next room a great feast awaits.

EMPTY CHAIR

vodun altar

The chair does not touch the ground. Chains and ropes lace the back of the chair to the beams, to a cross, of concrete, empty bottle on one wing, a bottle wound in bright red threads on the other. As if one might be crucified sitting down.

The cross rises from some foundational chunk in a tool shed in Haiti, some slab, some altar stone white paint may have spilled over. But no white paint spilled from the cross, not, at least, from its final flourish. The cross now is black.

On the seat of the empty chair, a crumple of cloth. (Could be a bathing suit.) Under the hovering chair, a small coffin. And burned, painted, or carved into the wood at the head, still another cross. A shovel slants against a plain fence.

Such an odd, arbitrary vision of eternal life, two lines, one horizontal, one vertical, intersecting. But then, as Lenny Bruce said, if Christ had been put to death in the twentieth century, Catholic schoolgirls would kneel and pray with tiny electric chairs strung from their necks.

Outside, it's night. The fence twisted, more propped up than set in the ground. A bright yellow wall is blowing away. The crossbeam branches that hold up the roof point toward the vast Haitian night. Night, into which the seated one ascended. Night in which a god might take a throne, so offered.

All is drenched in emptiness: the cardboard box on what passes for a bench, under it, the bright red crate of drained bottles around where the light is brightest. Where walls glow with the light needed for the camera.

Above all, strung banners, orange, blue, pink, yellow, triangles, cloth, or plastic, clustered. On the left, as if withdrawing from the shadow side where the shovel leans, its blade against the altar's base, as if to tip it over, pry it from off the face of the earth.

This could almost be a Mediterranean holy site, an arrangement of items in Syria or Egypt, 2nd century. Multiple belief systems are at work in the details. So is salvation effected in uncertain times. A vacated cross rises in a rain forest. New trees jump from rotting trunks.

The cross should be supporting beams ready for raising up a Logan airport parking garage. Weeks in the chipping yard, one summer, scraping excess concrete from the freshly poured slabs with coworker, Nibben O'Toole. Nibben liked to recall his time in the army. He praised Manila whorehouses. To accommodate demand, whores, he said, strung blankets between the cots. This made more rooms. All around rose happy sounds.

Whoever had a chance, would they not sit in that empty chair, take their place on that summit of becoming, a shovel on one side, on the other, a basket of bottles? Who would not be the new lord of an intoxicating and rotting world?

Amid the survivals of Dahomey, Yorba, and Catholic cultures, suspended, from the wing of the vodun altar cross, or behind it, framed by unlit Christmas lights, a vision out of yet one more mythology: an actress, famous photo, naked, wrapped in a huge snake, in what might have once been called the serpent of the skies. She's lying down, looking out, at Avedon, and beyond.

It's Nastassja Kinski. Long ago you used that name, Nastassja, for your new love. That was back in in 1982, in New York, the year *Cat People* came out.

A SELECTED GUIDE
TO THE FILMS OF NASTASSJA KINSKI

I. *Cat People* (1982)

First shot, a wide-branched tree, languorous panthers, a pillaged girl tied up, left for nightfall, so to copulate with a panther. Her descendants will be orphaned circus people, tended by a vodun priestess, Ruby Dee.

Somewhere, in the closing credits, a quote from Dante, *La Vita Nuova*. The quote tells of the transfiguring power of erotic obsession. Dante names his ultimate love, Beatrice, first seen by the poet in church at the age of nine.

During the movie someone must have quoted Dante in passing. Perhaps it was the incestuous brother of the visiting virgin who does not at first realize that she is also, deep down, though in human form as well, a panther. You don't remember any Dante. You play back the film and find none. Play back his tormented end, made by fate to mate with his sister, so to stop the murderous imperative that commands all who turn from human to panther, a metamorphosis brought on by sex, the desire for which, though the brother is an evangelical minister, he cannot overcome. He, Malcom McDowell, confronts his sister, Nastassja Kinski, with their true nature. She rebuffs him. She stabs his hand with a blade of broken glass.

The quote does not occur even where it might be expected, during the sex scenes. But you replay them anyway, replay when she looks in the mirror, horrified after having given in to her momentary love for a New Orleans zookeeper, and when she stands naked behind a window frame. Her breasts are covered by the crossbar. The dark narrative gnarl, brother, sister, and zookeeper, marks the start of her turning into a panther.

In a bayou at night she drops her white gown, glides naked, moonlit, through the trees. The camera shows the hallucinatory colors and angles which constitute her "Cat Vision." Having fled the side of a lover whom she has put off in defense of her still untrammeled chastity, she stalks a rabbit, her breasts, back, and abdomen sinuous in the bluish light.

The Dante quote, never found, is part of the film's decadent aesthetic, along with the snakes, the cat statues perched on the roof of the zoo at night that give it the air of a temple, the flashes of religious icons, the lascivious statues in the park, the Last Supper print on a whorehouse wall. Given the actress, that double of a doomed past love, a missing page of *La Vita Nuova,* seems cruelly perfect.

Malcom McDowell can only go on, picking up prostitutes in New Orleans cemeteries, having sex, turning into a panther, ravaging the prostitutes, so that death can give him back a human form, until he's finally shot. His sister, Nastassja Kinski, the image of the soul trapped on Earth, ends up a panther, caged at the zoo by the zookeeper whom she loves, and who loves her, all while he pursues a romantic relationship with a redhead.

II   *Exposed* (1983)

The blackboard has the title of another film written on it, *A Touch of Evil.* Lecturing on *The Sorrows of Young Werther,* reciting lines from Goethe, the professor looks at his student, Nastassja Kinski. She does not look impressed. She's about to break up with the professor, about to quit the snowbound Midwestern college. She's destined for New York City. The camera's on her face. The professor is talking about the Angel of Death.

In New York, Kinski's character, Elizabeth, becomes a famous model. She poses in a fluffy coat before the World Trade Center. She poses in Paris. She interacts, there, with terrorists already familiar from explosions that open the film. At a gallery showing photographs of Elizabeth, an art critic notes her likeness to Garbo, Lombard, and Monroe. "Different clothes. Different selves," someone at the exhibit remarks. A photographer who seems to know something notes: "Pretty on the outside, trouble underneath."

More and more as the movie runs on, exposition is suppressed. Scenes become dreamlike. Elizabeth drifts into unreal entanglements. Social interactions are so incoherent they seem, instead, highly stylized. Elizabeth is exposed. But also, the world is exposed to Elizabeth. On the street Rudolph Nureyev approaches her. He is reciting a poem by William Carlos Williams. She hears and follows him. He, a world-renowned concert violinist, is on a secret mission to destroy the previously introduced terrorists. The terrorists are led by none other than Harvey Keitel. Nureyev says he, Nureyev, is a child of atrocity tracking down those who killed his mother.

At this point the movie crosses into pure dream. Only this can explain the most erotic moment in the film. Nureyev caresses Elizabeth with the bow of his violin. (Critics are divided. The scene may or may not be based on a Dali painting.) Elizabeth's sexual passion has been intensifying for a while, at least since her sexy, solitary dance in her room when she waved her red jacket before the horns of her exercycle, as if she were a matador.

Effortlessly, Elizabeth infiltrates the terrorist organization. They're planning to bomb a train station. She engages the terrorists in something like philosophical debate. At some point one of them, making a crucial distinction, says: "I'm not talking about manners; I'm talking about destruction."

The terrorist mastermind, Harvey Keitel, has on hand
a copy of *Cosmo.* Elizabeth is on the cover. Harvey Keitel says
he has studied her face, as if to make overt the barely suppressed
angelology that rules the film. The reason for your coming, he
says, is to cause my death. Elizabeth, Nastassja Kinski, tears to
pieces the *Cosmo* cover. "In what you call Creation," Harvey
Keitel tells her, "there's nothing left."

III *To the Devil a Daughter (1976)*

Having chosen the perfection of man over the perfection
of God, Father Rainer finds himself excommunicated. Rather
than repent, he pursues his Gnostic inclinations. Pledged to
Astrogoth, he plans to call up the dark lord, out of the beyond,
and into the flesh.

All this time, Nastassja Kinski has been raised as a nun in
Bavaria. But the evil hour is at hand. The innocent, beautiful teenage
nun leaves the continent for London. She is unaware of her place in
Father Rainer's plan for loosing demonic forces on the world.

It turns out Nastassja Kinski, his daughter, through
a pact over the bloodied altar made from a childbed and the
corpse of his wife, has been pledged to Satan. Father Rainer, her
demonic father, celebrates his birthday just as Sister Catherine,
Nastassja Kinski, arrives in London. Sister Catherine sleepwalks
through swinging sixties London. In his demonic cell in a
mortuary on a pentagrammic table, Father Rainer arranges
magical plates. In this way he calls Nastassja Kinski to him.

Richard Widmark, though a renowned debunker of
spiritual fraud, cannot protect the innocent young nun who, in
life, is the daughter of the maniacal German actor beloved of
Werner Herzog, Klaus Kinski, when she drives a letter opener
into the head of a luckless literary agent. Black magic is at work.

Widmark visits the bishop. Taken to a well-guarded library of heretical texts, he reads the book of Astrogoth. He learns that the fate of the fallen world is at stake.

The wicked ex-priest must, with magical semen, beget upon Nastassja Kinski a fiend. In a white nightgown the virginal nun lies before the altar of Astrogoth. An icon depicts a priapic satyr nailed to an upside down cross. When Father Rainer, who could only have been played by Christopher Lee, makes love to Nastassja Kinski, each of their faces takes on, in turn, the golden mask of the evil divinity.

Like a sheriff in a western, Richard Widmark, the American occultist, moves through a late symbolist fantasia. He's like John Wayne shambling through a film of *Les Fleurs du mal*. Richard Widmark has got to save the girl. He knows that flint dipped in blood will protect him from the demons when he steps inside the circle of blood to disrupt the ultimate world-concluding ritual. But he'd rather duke it out.

An elegant and well-spoken Christopher Lee offers Richard Widmark the chance to have Sister Catherine. Richard Widmark hallucinates. The camera marks this with a kind of visual reverb. Nastassja Kinski steps out of her white robe. She walks toward him in slow motion. The voluptuousness of the fourteen-year-old nun is at last revealed. The power she will have as the incarnation of the devil is offered to Richard Widmark. Widmark hardly seems Christlike enough to wave away her nakedness.

IV   *Tess* (1979)

In *Tess*, Nastassja Kinski returns to Stonehenge where she had appeared a few years before, also at the conclusion of a film. This time she's clothed, exquisitely, in a full-length, bloodred dress, hat, veil. She's just murdered the man who had raped her. Seeping through the floor of the seaside boarding house where she had become his mistress, his blood stains in the white of the downstairs parlor ceiling.

A pre-Christian paganism rules this world. The director Roman Polanski delights in it. Early on a stone marks the site of a brutal killing. Polanski has Tess kneel before it. Kinski is the living spirit of the pastoral landscape, the world of harvesting, milking dairy cows, and crude country courtships done in colors from Millet and Corot. At times the film seems to stop just so the cinematographers can honor Kinski's beauty. In the end she lies on a slab of pagan stone. The light of modernity's dawn betrays her. Police on horseback approach through the mist.

In high school the English teacher described at length the hatred heaped on Hardy. They threw stones at him. Everyone in England wanted Tess to die for having sex outside of marriage, he said. There at the poor cousin of Groton School, at a boarding school on the verge of financial collapse, the teacher said how much he detested Christianity. He talked about Greek tragedy. He talked about Dionysus. He talked about how cruel her fate, how horrible her end, how the world's hatred of him and his hatred of the world made Hardy give up writing and turn to poetry.

Before she ever made a film, you were dreaming of Nastassja Kinski, weren't you? Her beauty in the film confirmed, no, no, it vastly exceeded, the beauty you had imagined in your lonely autumnal reading. You can see this in her eyes, her long dark hair. She was already there in your head, her distinct gaze, her gaze, which is the central event in *Tess*, as Roman Polanski clearly recognized. You thought you were her truer angel; you would rescue her, and you and the Tess-to-be, Nastassja Kinski, would live together in a great country house. But she was in fact the angel, did you not immediately sense that? She was the angel who had fallen into this world, suffering so terribly, enduring scorn and rejection, to find you, with her limpid grey eyes, pale face, with a small scar on her cheek.

In several of her films Nastassja Kinski appears to be in a trance. She passes through appearances looking and wondering, as if she just arrived from some far-off angelic realm or is rousing herself from one dream to enter a deeper one, ringed, in this instance, by harvest dances, virginal maids in white, wheat wreathes in their hair. She wanders through the tomb of the D'Urbervilles, a crypt in the shadow of which her dispossessed family camps in the gutter. She sees effigies in armor, clutching swords. Her trance deepens. Attentive, incredulous, she is the soul condemned to be in a body.

Conservative Polish Catholic theologians denounce Roman Polanski as a Gnostic. He depicts the soul, in this instance, Nastassja Kinski, betrayed by her angel who is in fact a demon. Only in death will she at last be loved. Kinski submits, then, ever more profoundly, to the trance of being tricked by fate, by beauty, by the illusions of the life where knowledge only increases, yes, sorrow, but above all, incredulity.

Early on, at the dance in the pasture, the girls, all in white, enact an archaic pattern that might as well be on a fragment of Greek pottery. The girls are hoping to be asked to dance by the loutish aristocrats who happen by, who despite her beauty pass by Nastassja Kinski. Does she see in that early choral interlude, in the pasture, filmed at the golden hour, the hell that will happen to her? She's swept into the underworld by her lordly rapist. The beauty of the world will come to exist to the degree she is in it but not of it. Or perhaps more horribly, only ever of it, in her blood red dress, asleep on an ancient altar, which Hardy compares to a wind-harp.

V   *Revolution* (1985)

Of the notable cast – Al Pacino, Donald Sutherland, the
singer Annie Lennox – only one actor grasps that the film they
are all in, *Revolution*, is a retelling of William Blake's apocalyptic
poem, *America a Prophecy*. Writers, producers, director,
showrunners, are clueless. Only Nastassja Kinski knows. This
knowing is the exact anguish she brings. This knowing is why her
feelings exceed what the movie offers as a cause for her tormented
gaze, her revolutionary rage, and her frequently erratic life choices.

By this point in her career, Kinski has accepted that she'll
always be cast as the nonplatonic soul lost in the world of matter.
She's accepted such a soul will often appear to be an angel from
some overthrown celestial hierarchy. In *Revolution*, she's neither
the Angel of Death nor the Angel of Redemption. The opening
scene: she steps down from a carriage in high aristocratic array, as
if the carriage were not in Boston but in Paris, twenty years later,
during a world-historical bloodbath for justice.

Incongruities flare. The film splices in another prophecy,
"The French Revolution." When Kinski steps down from the
carriage she steps onto an earth of universal insurrection. The
rampaging Bostonian rabble who tear off the head of a statue of the
king and throw it in the harbor are also beheading, in advance, the
French king. Two revolutions happen at once, both brought about
by that "Yankee bitch" Nastassja Kinski, pale, tremulous, eyes
looking on the day as if she's wept through the night.

As ever, the actress is otherworldly. She is the
angelophany of Al Pacino, who, an 18th century fur trapper
caught up, against his will, in the upheaval of the American
Revolution, some critics say, is miscast. Nastassja Kinski, however,
is unquestionably the perfectly embodied beauty of enlightened
revolutionary tendencies. She could have been painted by Elihu

Vedder. She steps into and out of scenes like an eerie, forsaken grief-struck angelic nomad full of sexy, revolutionary rage.

Toward the end of the movie, Kinski reveals herself to be the Angel of Revolution. History, fulfilling itself, is about to be no more. Kinski, with a liberated black house servant at her side, drives a supply cart in a snowstorm to Valley Forge and happens, there, to see her love Al Pacino again. Pacino has become a Native American scout leading Huron braves against his nemesis, Donald Sutherland, a British officer whose beloved son dies in his arms on a beach.

VI *Inland Empire* (2006)

The ad features the name Nastassja Kinski, though she does not appear in the film. Watched it twice, can't find her. Then, lost in the closing apotheosis, behind the cascading credits, as the players all return and sing, there she is, silent, happy, her face distinct for a few seconds. Beside the one who has journeyed far and suffered horribly, Laura Dern, Kinski takes a seat.

The two women on a couch in a parlor. Kinski, whose only appearance this is, fulfills the role of "The Lady." Amid the phantasmagoria of the feminine that the film is, she has no real rivals for this role, a role not played until the world of the film concludes, a conclusion over which she can be said, however enigmatically, to preside.

As for Laura Dern, however, the film presents so many incarnations that all women, perhaps all men and all women, could be avatars of someone else. In *Inland Empire* Dern plays an actress cast in the remake of a cursed Polish film, a film never completed. The actors who play the lovers were murdered back in Poland. By the end of *Inland Empire*, which breaks down then reasserts the line between life and art, over and over, neither Dern nor the audience can be sure whether a scene is in the movie within the movie, or is the movie itself, which stands, here, for life.

It is puzzling why such a well-known actor, and one with such occult associations as has been, in this *Selected Guide*, undeniably established, would, given scant screentime in a three-hour fantasia of female abjection, only appear in the final shot. Did David Lynch not know what he was doing, as some of his remarks seem to suggest? Does the murkiness of the digital camera reflect his state of mind? Or could it be that Nastassja Kinski is, in fact, the central figure of the film? She doesn't appear because she does not need to appear. When she does appear, in a coda that is, credits rolling, outside the film proper, amid characters joining in a frenzied ecstatic dance featuring a mesmerizing singer who also does not appear in the film, Nastassja Kinski does not say anything. She does not need to speak.

All women in the film are Nastassja Kinski. Laura Dern, both as Nikki and as Susie, the Hollywood Boulevard hookers, the eerie Polish woman early on at Dern's door who places a curse upon her, are emanations of the unseen Kinski. The tearful and trembling woman watching all on a screen, watching both the film and the film within the film, the "Lost Girl," is a furtherance of Kinski. The labyrinthine rooms, the corridors, the terrifying night-light, the hallucinatory rabbits enacting the civilities of a tragically distant domestic normalcy, the murderous men, the true inland empire, not real estate outside LA, but Poland, a nightmare Poland ruled by carnival freaks, gypsies, sadistic patriarchs, in short the whole Expressionist world that Lynch cinematically summons and abandons, it is all a waking dream of Nastassja Kinski, and a dream dreamed by Nastassja Kinski.

Laura Dern dies horribly, a street whore stabbed with a screwdriver on Hollywood Blvd. She staggers over the star of Dorothy Lamour. She falls amid the indigent, vomits blood, dies.

Have we reached the ultimate worldly emanation of a deified Nastassja Kinski? Now that the truest version of Kinski is dying, in life and not in art? The camera pulls back. There's a second camera. We are on the set of *No More Blue Tomorrows*, the remake of the cursed Polish movie.

Dern is alive in the film within the film, but within the larger film, the film that now includes both life and death, *Inland Empire*, she has entered an afterlife.

The camera wanders through a shadowy backlot arriving where Nastassja Kinski, the Queen of Death, who is all others yet always herself, who is beyond being known, who might be a goddess in a Hindu theophany, filling the plane of the visual, smiling, her face only visible for a moment, in the parlor, sits on the couch beside Laura Dern, together watching the forms of appearance dance before them.

LOST NOTEBOOK

It nags you, this loss, this drifting away of your only true possession, this amnesia you now live with, this dispirited wonder at the fate of your once-upon-a-time fastidiously noted interiority. Was there a thought there, the shadow of a thought, some icy chunks, some stones of a yet to be excavated thought, once meteoric, once lunar, once planetary, scattered in a blast, your lost pages the only proof a blast happened. Your words were remnants shooting through the depths, as it were, of space, caught passing by the earth, should conceptual pebbles and intelligible dust so pass there, caught by the lens of the outpost of the notebook, your migrant observatory, phenomena caught, jotted there, far from the celestial palaces wandered through in dreams. Perhaps only the glowing debris that charts the faded trajectory of a thought, a true thought, not those ragtag notions of others, hobbled together, and for so long, because you wanted, for a mollifying duration, to astonish. Those great phrases, as if yours, they would stun your priests and teachers. Though to be candid, you were not good in school. Minuses trailed after your Bs like a keenly drawn line across your transcript, like a line that would void a check. Your professor, the author of *The Moral Rules*, remember him? He called you in about a paper labored over eighteen hours straight, handwritten, in pencil, in the all-night library study, where you sat across from the most beautiful and brilliant woman you had ever seen, a fellow student. It was introductory class, but certainly, you were beyond it. You had jumped over the assignment, Freshman though you were, and moved directly to the matter of your own personal philosophy. Soon summoned, were you expecting an invite to an advanced class, one that would critique and demolish what was broadly understood to be Western metaphysics? You thought he called you in for you to be acclaimed. Instead, he asked if when you wrote your paper you were high on drugs. If you were not high, he reasoned, you were very, very depressed. He asked you, the distinguished author of *The Moral Rules*, a work which established in Reason the Ten Commandments, if you considered yourself depressed. He asked were you having trouble with life away from home. He said that before he would entertain any further academic work on your part, you would need to see a counsellor. He said he would not accept any more work from you without a note from a mental health counsellor. They were good, he said, specially trained, and were kept available on campus at some expense, paid for by the college, for emotionally ill students who found themselves in your situation.

ROADSIDE HELMET

for Ed Roberson

The gold of the face of the
The gold of the face of the helmet,
motorcycle helmet, side of highway,
face of the helmet, visor a gold visor,
face of the helmet but no helmet,
gold visor no helmet, no motorcycle,
no rider without a visor riding
a motorcycle, riding on a road,
one might imagine, in sunlight.
Gold of the visor, from which,
dare we deduce, a gold helmet.
Presumed gold of an unseen helmet
worn while, how can it not be,
riding on a gold motorcycle?
Empty highway. How is it I'm
walking here, no cars, no trucks,
no military vehicles, no motorcycles
in sight. Nothing much in sight
but a visor, blown off the face,
a gold veil, pulled off the face.
The visor over the face of the rider,
cracked, scraped, fissures across
the face of whoever, is it you,
Hermes, messenger from beyond,
rode a motorcycle through the world
in daylight or at night? World
as seen through a cracked visor
of, possibly, a gold motorcycle
helmet at night. Possibly. Come
to think of it, more silver than gold.
(Much depends on the light.)

Cracked, not shattered, the
face of the helmet, the visor.
Thought it gold. It seems silver.
Somewhere the rider of the gold
or silver motorcycle speeds along
bare faced, tears streaming,
from grief or joy, or just the wind
blowing from beyond, having
left a message, or is still out there,
bearing word, to whatever world
he passes into, after this one.

RULE OF THUMB

Seen him be so. Seen him send friendships up in flames.
To get along with Bob, imagine you have a sister. Imagine you
have an emotionally damaged sister. Then, anything you're about
to say to Bob, before you say it, ask yourself, would I say this to
my emotionally damaged sister? Would this upset, send into
cataclysmic and deeply destructive rage, plunge into a paralyzing,
suicidal abyss, my sister, my emotionally damaged sister? Before
any word is said, ask: will this touch upon some element of
the emotional damage suffered by my sister, suffered once, and
emphatically still suffering? Before you talk, think of your sister,
your once beautiful, younger sister. Think before the damage,
how fun she was. Think of her birth, the day she came home
from the hospital. Your parents let you hold her. Feel again the
deep joy that filled the house. Remember her look, her innocent
laugh. Then remember the start of her hard lessons that so pained
you, and still pain you to see her endure. To get by with Bob,
have the fact of such a sister, or some analogous situation, always
in mind. Remember: the imperceptible is all Bob sees. Affronts
hide in any aside. Never name anyone he knows. (Never say you
know me.) Avoid drawing upon your own experience. Here's
a rule of thumb: take what you would say, be tempted to say,
go over it with great care. Set words before Bob like jewels on a
platter, like gems brought some far distance, like gifts brought by
Wise Men across a desert. After an exchange with Bob, there may
arise feelings of warm rapport. That's fine but keep quiet. Always
ask, have I forgotten, am I forgetting, my sister, the crest and
plunge of her moods. Fine awhile, then came damage. She found
herself to be damaged. Found herself to be greatly damaged.
Then she destroyed the household. Recall her resentment, her
loneliness, her extravagant, perilous gestures. Bear in mind her
retaliations, you never saw them coming. Review how fathomless
the depth of her hatred, her zeal in destroying any sentiment

which would favor reciprocity. Spare a care for the emotional damage of your emotionally damaged sister. Ask, again, how the damage happened. Wasn't she fine one day, a disaster the next? Go over that before you start talking to Bob. Talking to Bob is a road. No one on such a road can turn around once Bob starts listening. To be honest, that you are numbered among Bob's friends should cause you concern. Yes, it's great to be a friend of Bob. He's capable of great magnanimity. If you say nothing, he could be a lifelong friend, an emotionally damaged lifelong friend, one who could turn on you in an instant. Keep your mouth shut. That's how to be a true friend to Bob. After all, this is how you made life bearable for your sister, your emotionally damaged sister. This is how you become the one who is emotionally damaged. This is how you forget your role as the one who does not upset her. This is how you forget to keep your mind racing just ahead of hers. This is how you forget to live in advance of what is always about to happen.

PICTURE MOURNING

for Rob Sikorski

Dead faces in a photo.

Photo in the hands of the living.

Dead face, trick of light,
as are the hands of the living.

Hands, in photos, holding

photos of faces.

Living faces looking
at, away from, the dead.

*

The smile of the fireman
in his uniform, like
he's at a parade, held
in the hands of his son.

Behind the son the widow
half draped in a flag.

*

The beautiful face of the dead
guerilla fighter, Anea Sin.
Long black hair over one eye,
a wisp across the throat,
lips parted, sensuous,
reproachful, as if to say:
"In a just world my picture
would be in a college yearbook,
or a modelling portfolio.
It would not be here, held aloft,
on placards, in a crowd of
raised fists, red banner,
a liberation sash across
those gathered in the street,
at the festival of a martyr,
who turns out to be me,
handfuls of flowers floating
beneath my floating face."

*

A flash in the darkness.

Flash of a clear face held up
by a child on an Egyptian street.

As if torn from a sheet of
wallet-sized photos,

like when the photographer
comes to school on a certain day.

You pick out a background,
hand him a check.

Dead Egyptian boy.

Scarf, ski sweater, triangle
peaks rising across his chest.

*

The faces float in darkness.

They're like postage stamps
commemorating Osiris.

The hands of the grievers
hold up a stamp as if to ask:

"Now, where is the letter,
the letter I 've been writing
since this death?

Usually, I write a letter
and can't find the stamp.

But in this instance,
the stamp is all I can find."

*

But looking at some of
the bereft, those in veils,
it feels like it's the living
who've gone away,

who are in a place
beyond writing
and receiving letters.

*

A woman at the anti-police
rally holds up a picture

of Amadou Diallo.

Man behind her, also in black.

On her shoulder, his hand.

He's also holding up
a face, but more casually,

like it's a ticket, a parking pass,
a grocery list on the back
of a mass mailing.

The woman's hand
turns the photo
toward her heart.

As if the face, the
image of the face,
has arisen out of it,
out of her heart.

As if the picture had
come to rest just beneath
the edge of the veil

flowing down over
her black parka.

As if she were about to
gently blow on it,

on the face of the man
beaten to death by police.

As if, with her breath,
he might come back,
live again, if only
as a ghost, or a dream.

*

As did a young man in
a photo from Pakistan, who
appeared to his mother as
she herself lay near death.

He wore a scarf draped
over his shoulder. He gave
the scarf to his mother, told
her to wrap it around her.

She did. She felt warmth
move through her body.
Days later, the illness left her.
She never dreamed of him again.

*

In the Land of Lament,
the land of Rilke's "Ninth Elegy,"
the faces of the dead glow
with life, like these faces, these
with futures to behold.

*

The faces float free of
the hands that offer them
to our witness, faces bright
as candles set in paper boats
at night, loosed on the river,
a small, brilliant fleet,
voyagers who have left,
and left us behind, like
women in antiquity
ululating in the hills.

*

Look at the faces of the man and woman
holding up pictures of their sons,
the freedom fighters.
The curator of the exhibit
notes in a pamphlet
how often the pictures
of the dead, within
the memorial pictures,
seem cut out from
the local paper,

as if the now dead
were still a student
who has won an award,
or got first in a competition
and gone on to compete
on the national level.

In this instance, one son
seems scholarly, abstract,
lost in thought, not there,
like he's running some
equation in his head.

The other brother is
brusque and muscular,
more like a Greco-Roman
wrestler, no doubt as tough
as he looks. He looks like
he knows he could
pin you in five seconds.

The large, framed photos
of the two dead sons stand
like doors, behind which
stand the parents.

The parents have stepped,
are stepping, are about to
conclude stepping,

through the door of
death, just as their sons,
the freedom fighters,
have stepped through a door,
have entered the house of death.

The mother's eyes are wet.
Her skin's fresh, at odds
with her grey hair, black
blouse, aged hands, as if
aging happened in
this exact moment.

She sees the boat
to the underworld
as it's passing by.

Her sons are on it.
They don't recognize her.

The boat is full of
freedom fighters
from Azerbaijan.

The slain are happy
to see each other!

*

A picture white as
as a field of fresh snow.

One can barely make out
the dead face in a square like
a large blank sketch pad.

The title of the photo:

"My Biggest Brother,
Everett, Who Killed
Himself When We Came
Back From Vietnam."

In the photo within
the photo the barely
visible Everett looks
even younger than
the bereaved boy
who is his brother.

Everett's little brother
stands, dressed in black,
against a white wall.

*

The ice storm glare of
the photo that frames
the photo blends into
the gallery's white wall
which almost wipes
from all record the
bewildered, bereft,
with sharp black eyes,
living sibling, looking
like he has wandered
into stage lights and
forgotten his lines.

*

Considered as dying stars,
these faces should let no
light escape them.

*

At a World Trade vigil
holding up photos
while carrying staves
from an agrarian world,
maybe in the mountains of Peru,
like they came to perform
some ancient ritual
in a modern city,
a family is looking
around for room enough
in the rush hour crowd
to perform a dance.

*

A poster of a recent martyr
is put up the day after his death.

The poster had been printed
in advance of the death.

Multiple martyrs,
like ads for the circus
or a rock show opening

on Broadway,

plaster the plywood
that hides from view
the construction site.

A little window.

Pedestrians can look down
into the massive hole,

see the first of the girders,
the welder's sparks.

*

Edge of a face lost to blackness.
Downcast eyes, black shawl,
shawl more of a shroud.

This photo, is this in India?
Is this in the city of widows,
where clothing stores
only carry black?

*

The last photo an interior,
yet wind is blowing.

Heavy lines in her face,

thick lashes, rings beneath
the eyes, bedraggled hair
over her forehead.

The woman is
deeply indoors.

Church, mosque, tomb.
A blur of brightness,
a votive flame.

She's a shade,
a living funereal
sculpture.

The hand of hers that
holds up the face of
her turbaned son,
ring, deep wrinkles.

She is with us in the land of
the living, but then she
drops into shadows.

WHERE AFFECTION HOLDS
NO STEADY MANSION   IV

eleven laments

I

Amid such a gala
the long parted,

secretly
torrid –

*

Would she were forever
stepping into the

ballroom from
the grey of

evening,
the colors in the

play of her
gown

so
dazzling.

*

Though
acting more like

local nobility receiving
dignitaries who

keep
arriving

amid the music, flowers
and wafting, savory trays,

poised
greetings.

     *

No cupped, hot mouth
          close to an ear –

     *

Within the purview
of this vast celebration

the discretely passionate two
confide only

intermittently,
quietly, but not

noticeably
hushed.

*

All of what
touched each in

in the intervening
years, the confession

that would be
an ecstasy of

telling, can only
be intimated.

II

Yet another final farewell a fan of
his unfolding hand across

her temple,
back, then away,

the hair threading
between three

crooks of
four fingers.

III

White curtains,
rippling and falling

flat against the
windows

across from which
a bed, glimmering,

as if silver threads slipped
through sheets,

blankets,
pillowcases,

though the coverlet is dark blue
and, left out at its

exact center
a notebook,

the one, it'd seem, about
which she was

so secretive
years back

before, that
is, her

elusiveness,
over decades of

distance,
became what

it is now, an
absolute

absence, the
notebook left open.

IV

Perhaps, after all,
your love is still alive,

having not,
in her lapse

from all daylight
connaissance,

died, merely
taken up

a new
body.

                  *

            (A tiger, panther,
            snow leopard, this

bounding
bright flash,

is what she
must be now.)

V

Not at all enough time
to bury his face in

waves of
her black hair.

No time at all for
a few tears

to sink through
her hair to her neck.

*

Emissaries from sleep's
deeper regions

whisk her away,
just as she says,

"As it's unlikely
we'll meet

in waking life
again, whatever

you write from
now on it

should be
a love letter

addressed
to me, This

spirit (Feel free
to think of

him as
Hermes)

will give you
my email

address
in hell."

*

But then, you
have difficulty,

it seems, in
simply

taking down

the address, the

beginning and end of
all art, given to

you by, quite
possibly,

the god of dreams
and of writing.

*

It's all numbers.
It's very long.

The ink won't hold.
The shape of an eight's

too complex. The
five smears. The three

starts clear but
loops into

an inky gnarl of
failing intelligibility.

Hermes takes
pity, takes

out "magic paper
from Pakistan."

hands it to you.
One side's

rough as tree bark,
the other's silky.

"Such paper is
meant only

for use," he
says, "in

mislived lives
like yours."

       *

Dip the bristle into
the uncapped jar

The silver flow of the ink
is beautiful, welling

and tapering across
the forest shades and

shadows of the
magic paper.

       *

(And so, this first trial
this initiation into

poetic art leads
less to passion than to

dazzlement:
the ink runs

wild down the
page in a brilliant

mercurial
drizzle.)

*

Despite your despair
Hermes hints at

one last hope:
"I don't know

where she is
I don't even know

her last name
anymore

she changed that
after the two

of you
destroyed

each
other.

But I do
know this:

she' s now
called *Elaina.* "

VI

The receding waters having left
spatters of gleaming pools

in what had once
been basements.

The shadowy hole
appearing just ahead

turned out to be
a pedestrian tunnel

suddenly familiar, leading
to the time and place

of the waking
present.

She looks right
back at him this time

and stops
walking.

VII

Fabulously dressed
couples step from cabs.

Revolving door.
In the lobby

an art opening
is in full swing.

Visible through the
whirling glass, spotlit,

mounted on a wall,
a chunk of mashed metal,

once, possibly,
the hood of a car,

black valleys of
shadow,

small floor lights
trained on the crushed,

buckled panel,
and peeling paint

lighting up
silvery creases

and folds
of steel.

VIII

Zebra-striped dress.
Around the waist, a black band

pressing a gold
medallion against

her womb. Turns out,
all these years

she's been in
New Orleans . . .

*

At night in front of
her new favorite club.

"Forget the crowd!
Let's go in!" (And what

bouncer, in New York
or the world, could

ever defy
her wishes?)

*

Her arms, as ever,
gesturing as

you both enter, music,
spices and

hypnogogic lights
filling the air,

swift, abrupt, ever
reconfiguring angles

glimmering
bracelets, bangles

at her ear, on this
clear evening,

ever more
subtle

implications
arising around

whatever she was,
again, as ever

before,
arms flying,

in the midst
of saying.

IX

A tower rising
from a forested ridge.

A tower like those used for power lines
though this one kept going,

into the clouds.
Lithe and nimble

she led their climb
up a long service ladder

higher and higher
above the ridge top.

Arriving at
a mesh of metal,

a station, of sorts, above
an immense valley

fields and houses
mountains on the horizon,

they rest before they
entered the low clouds,

cross-legged, curling
into each other,

each with an arm
looped to one of the

metal strips that
made up the dizzying

wisp of a tower
so much beauty

a valley, a river, a plain
the edge of the earth

they would leave
together for good,

and the flame of
the horizon.

X

From the hubbub of
airport security procedures

as he files towards
departure

for a second
he sees her face

amid the deplaning
amid the

dispersing
arrivals.

XI

Waking, you could taste on your lips,
lifetimes back, that black lipstick.

IMAGINED DIALOGUE

I said: a slate hangs from my neck.
You said: on it is written,

could you read it,
your every last sin.

I said: so, what, now,
where you are, is

your favorite color?
You said: all

prisms are
a prison.

I said: tradition
forbids the wine be

tasted until
evening.

You said: the cup is
at my lips, now.

I said: I see what
Love allows.

You said: your eyes,
tell me, are they

closed or
open?

REVEALED, REVEILED

a suite for Randy Hayes

I

Huge Buddhas in cellophane.

In this world, things that appear most
clearly conceal other things,

or stand between, or float over, or slip through,

as the tree blocks out the mountain,
or the blaze of the sun paints
the surface of the lake.

Waves lost in their own candescence
but the shadows of the waves –
hardly more than ripples,

they seem to seethe.

The page of a book is folded over.

Sleek and smooth through a slit
in the skirt, the transvestite's thigh.

Clarity proclaims hiddenness.
The seen is never complete.

Petals floating in a votive bowl
conceal the translucence of the water.

The divinities are wrapped in cloth,
bound with rope around waist,

neck, and hands, like hostages
in a film about terrorism.

In India, drying linen covers low shrubs.

In Ellensburg, WA, a young girl in a T-shirt
– faded image of a reggae singer –
leads a blind horse through a parking lot
cluttered with pick-ups and teepees.

Looking down, she appears solemn.

In the Netherlands, a bike draped
in dried leaves leans against a brick wall.

In Mississippi, a cabin is devoured by ivy.

In Bangkok, Buddhas packed in peeling tinfoil.

In a summer palace in Beijing, the statue of
a dragon is bound in chicken wire.

In many, many, places around the world
architecture is lost behind scaffolds.

A section of Westminster Abbey.
The dome of a mosque in India.
A huge gateway in Inner Mongolia.
In Amsterdam, a wall of the Magna Plaza.
In Rome, the tomb of Augustus.

So too several floating restaurants in Hong Kong.
Squibs of piping and planks under huge sheets
as if a magician were about to make
the whole world disappear.

A lion. A woman. A tank. A fluttering bird.

A receptor dish is glimpsed atop a palace.

In Mozambique, mask on his face,
a man with a weed whacker.

In Seattle, a hooker pulls a vinyl miniskirt
further down over her upper thighs.

Thailand is a huge outdoor chessboard at night.

A smiling guard stands among chess pieces
wrapped for the night in clear plastic,

though it seems a few of the
thigh-high black pawns are not.

In Rome, pop singer Andy Williams,
at night in a plaza, before huge columns.

Massive black door, spectators held back by ropes.

Movie lights turn Andy Williams pure white.
So, too, the hairdresser who walks behind him,
So, too, the umbrella the hairdresser
holds over the head of Andy Williams.

In the lobby of a Beijing hotel, stone
and marble in elegant swirls, on the floor
by the staircase, a large black urn.

The urn is behind the piano,
but from this distance the urn
seems on top of the piano,

as if it held the ashes of
a pianist or of a singer.

Three jackets hang on posts of
a fence around the Forbidden City.

In Jackson, Mississippi, at Dr. Duck's bait shop,
a sport utility van blocks out the sign
on the bait shop that begins:

Pawn Shop Cash Loans on Guns.

In London, behind shop glass,
rabbits dangle by their back feet.

Their upside-down bodies are partially lost
in the reflection of the street on the glass.

In the reflection is traffic,
a corner shop with letters reversed,
and possibly the shadow of
the photographer of all this,
shade heightening the clarity,

Randy Hayes, a ghost on the glass.

II

  e Eterna

  In whatever language, if the word is a word, there is an
e (long e) in front of it, *e eterna*. No *x* after it although an *ex*,
some last abiding frazzle of Latin, flashes in your brain. *Ex eterna*,
out of, away from, eternity, *ex eterna*, or is it formerly eternal?

Then, as the flame of white off-center left on the canvas comes toward you, you feel you can't stay in the uncertainty of *eterna*. You feel that, as you study the letters, the white light is getting close to you, whelming your vision. Turning to it, you can see that the sense of its being borne toward you has been confirmed. A figure carries it, a running child, bearing aloft a torch, a torch about to be handed on to you in a tragic relay you did not know you were a part of, the very torch carried by generations of runners through the hilly terrain of Asia Minor, a torch lit from the fires of Troy. Perhaps you are the lucky one who will carry the torch into the city. What city? The one where Clytemnestra waits for Agamemnon to return? This is the fire seen with a woeful shudder by the guard on the wall at the opening of the *Oresteia*, the guard who foresees what will befall and so is struck dumb. Since the messenger, here, is, in modern times, no more than a lampstand, some stay from grief is available. Still, there is word to be delivered, word that the world's most civilized city has fallen, that it is now gone, and we are still living the fall of Troy. But the word is not to be delivered till the spell is broken, the spell that imprisons the messenger in this painting, broken perhaps by Hermes himself, who more often leads souls *into* the eternal. Greyish blue takes on a tone of finality. The table lamp creates a shadow figure on the reflected whiteness of the tabletop. The figure less a god from antiquity than a vodun doll. The eternal may be a curse. Such speculation is belied by the calm and solidity of, at the bottom edge of the table, a book, and on or under the book's cover, a gondola. A gondola and a name, Monteverdi. The curse of the eternal gives way to dreams of a holiday, sight-seeing in Europe, and of a first-rate summer production of a popular opera. The dream book is leatherbound. You can feel in your fingers the pleasure of its heft, perhaps beneath the cold stone archway of a public monument with winged cherubs holding a wreath. Have we already read this book? Perhaps we are drowsy. The book's been set down beside the bed, here in this atelier overlooking a canal. Perhaps when reaching to turn off the light, we will find that our hand is that of Edith Warton or of Henry James. What have we been reading? The closed book is forever closed. But a book upper right corner is open to the title page: *La Secunda Part Della Geographia* Di CL Tolomeo.

III

as much as Randy said Randy as much as said

Randy as much as said: I have my own philosophy about the image. As the image darkens. Or brightens. Or becomes clear. Loss is happening. There are images behind the image. They fade. They are lost, yet these two things depend on each other. That's all. The beauty of the image, and then the other image that must be taken away. It's simple, but it took me a long time to understand.

On the anniversary of, for me, an overwhelming death, Randy said or as much as said: each grid is a veil. What Randy does is take photographs, hundreds, thousands, of photographs. He travels around the world, he walks around a city at night, bars, graveyards, convenience stores. He takes pictures of places and people in places and then he pins some of the pictures on a wall, in careful rows, in a grid. Then, since he is a painter, he paints some extraordinary scene on top of them.

Do you see that knotted curtain in a room in China, where a figure in a dark corner has her face in her hands and then you slowly notice a photographic image is there, where the paint thins, ghostly landscapes, portraits, hidden from view, they break in on her world, on your world, like a memories, like a piece of a past life, but a life that isn't yours? You never get to see your past lives because you don't live in one of my paintings. But then, Randy said or as much as said: a much-missed past life can vanishes as soon as it's seen. Maybe the lives that compose the veil of the grid is hers, the woman in a room in China. Maybe that's why she is grieving so deeply. Her life, her memories of all her lives, are gone in the brilliant colors of the present, yellows, blues, in the gold, in the green.

The paint on the photograph is also a veil, a veil that varies in its densities, in places almost translucent, a gold or blue wash in places as thick as a drop cloth, the realities that the photos render seems beyond any gaze forever, and yet one knows it's there, and if the painting were destroyed, could be seen. The painting defies us to destroy it, Randy said or as much as said: when I paint, I like to ask myself how badly do I want to see a true image of the world?

IV

Crucifixion in Silver at 10:19

The wall. The cross. The Christ. A silver-grey glance. As if stamped out in metal, not so bright a metal as to be ornamental, a few shades too grey. But after a moment, a warm grey – is there some blue in it? Some pink? Mixed-in traces of dawn or twilight? A moment more, the grey turns industrial, the tint of a lid or a bumper on the hull of an ocean-going ship.

A shadow between the crucified and the wall. The cross as if made in elementary school arts and crafts. Beams cut from cereal box cardboard. They recall that the vogue for breakfast cereal comes from the revivalist zeal of the 19th century. Then the beams are covered with wrinkly silver foil. Perhaps the cross is evolving into serious metalcraft, a sword, a shiv, something pounded into shape. The clock on the wall may be a photograph, may be the one photographic image in the painting. As such it achieves priority over the icon, so much larger, beside it.

Washed out, pale, almost swallowed by the wall, the clock dominates. It's Baudelaire's own crucifix, dividing time into the Calvary of the work week. At first the clock challenges the cross, historical time's triumph over ritual time. But the new, secular temporality reveals itself to be an intensified ancient and ongoing agony. The clock is the cross all mortals hang upon. The hour hand is sunk in the ground, the minute hand is a cross bar, the second hand is the centurion's spear.

Th time notation, 10:19, 25 seconds short of 10:20, is at odds with Gospel accounts. So, too, the execution. The arms of Christ have been broken off and removed. The hands are still nailed, at the wrists, to the cross. A red glow marks the left shoulder. There's a touch of red on the cross behind the head. It's strange to see those two hands like gloves hung up to dry on a clothesline, the hands that calmed the seas, that multiplied loaves and fishes, that drove out the moneychangers, that broke the bread, that healed the centurion's son.

V

No Cover

Window frame, huge squares of glass, nine all together, three rows, three per row. The bars of the window frame are white, though they absorb the color of the two sets of bright long neon tubes on either side, one hot pink, the other yellow.

Between these two zones of color, the exotic dancer, looking down, her head framed by the top middle window square. Her body is caught between the yellow and the pink. Her pink hand rests against the window crossbar. But her left hand that picks up so much of the yellow is open palmed, upraised as if pushing against the glass, her thumb hidden by another window cross bar.

In the mirrored door behind her, her reflection, back of legs, shoulders, back. Her ass is quartered by two bars of the outer window, the window she dances in, window looking out on a street in New Orleans. A man stands outside, eye-level with her feet. In profile, his shoulders half turned, as if he's about to walk away.

The window onto the street is the first frame within the actual frame. The nine panels of glass within the larger window are a grid over the dancing woman who looks down from the top center plane. The mirrored door frames her. The wall may also be mirrored. The bars of the outside window seem to be reflected within the window where the woman dances.

It may be a mistake to see her as dancing. She may just be stripping. Her knees are together, to one side. Both hands raised in front of her. One hand might be waving. the other seems to be deflecting or fending off or exerting control over the viewer, clearly not the man who has already looked and seems to be turning away. (So then, no one else but you.)

The center pane cuts off her head and hands and most of the legs below the hem of her very short black skirt. Her breasts are covered by a black bra with black string binding. Since she stands at an angle, her right breast is more exposed. It pours down into the black cloth. Her left breast, turned directly towards you, has touches of blue paint that sharpens the focus. Her eyes are hardly eyes, rather, smears of black paint that intensify her dominance. You feel the stripper sees you, though you cannot see her seeing you.

The eyes may be the window of the soul, but here, you're not allowed to look into them. Alone on a street in New Orleans, you look up and feel lost. A speculation is gathering, or rather, a bewilderment. On the breast so provocatively presented, are letters composed of electric bulbs, though many are burned out. The message is nonetheless legible. They spell out the name *Christ Jesus.*

CLASSICAL ANCESTOR

for Tony Sampas and Andrew Joron

The day's fret, the lunar eclipse
not visible, even from the glassed-in
rotating bar on the seventy-fifth floor,
sun falling in red-orange streaks,
slices of the sky aquamarine
with purplish crescents of clouds,
fading. All is as Kepler imagined
who, hundreds of years ago,
dreamed himself onto the moon.
Saw Earth sail across the sun.
It takes a great deal of thought
to see the earth as if from the moon
so that tonight we might find ourselves at
the narrow end of a cone of shadow,
a funnel of darkness, seeing
our origin, edged in red, sunrise
and sunset continuously
occurring at opposing ends,
the earth rising from fire then
arching back into burning darkness.
Unless, that is, we find ourselves
atop a hotel at the North Pole
where we are perfectly still
on the planetary axis and the sun
moves horizontally through the sky,
circles around us, never sets,
rather than here in Georgia,
where a red moon hides behind
a cloud bank, an ashen thumbprint
on the petals of the night's rose.
We call you and tell you and you

rush onto the porch, slip, fall
into a snowbank and find yourself
looking directly at the moon as
the shadow of the earth recedes,
and the moon goes through
a month in a moment, or so it
seems, crescent, to quarter, to half,
to three quarters, the curve of
earth visible on the moon.
So your ancestors the Greeks
knew the shape of the earth,
told to Aristotle by the curve
of that shadow. And he said:
"Now all we must do is find out
how vast it is, and what is on it,
and where it goes after it rounds
back here, and who we are,
who observe this, and where
does it all come from, us, the
moon, the shadows, the sun,
our eyes, our minds so eager
to know this immensity."

HECTIC ENDEAVOR

In military uniform at the airport.
When he'll be seen again, an open question.
The uniform a bright, deep blue,
fits him well though he's
slender, almost slight. Excited
about flying fighter jets
he consults a man pouring
water into a bowl on the floor
who says the divas have
fallen into the ground,
but now they are restless.

This is not the time for
seeds to stir, but the time
for the thought of seeds stirring.
A man and woman with masks
stand beside the bed.
A sleeper lies, oblivious.
Softly, the two speak to each other.
His mask is like a sheet of glass,
with forests, mountains and
streams painted on it.
She, however, has the mask of
a girl in a Gulag surviving
great sorrow. Yes, sleeper,
you vowed not to write
but you've broken that vow.

But then, you are merely one
through whom God's love passes.
You are the one means by which
a secret treasure is known,
as is the orange glow above

the trees that then fade into day.
There is no surprise if roses
are found in rose gardens,
Ibn Arabi said. The surprise
comes when roses spring
up in the pit of a fire.

*

Spring's close to exploding.
The woods wait while a grey,
aged, skeletal anorexic walks
with vigor on her path,
a medieval soul passing
pale each day through
the trees, daring any to doubt
she is as alive as alive is.
Still, the question presses
close: whose soul is she?
Each observing feels
bid to ask: "And where,
each afternoon, does *my*
soul walk? Through what
woods? Is it only in its absence
that I can be said to be free?"

*

The curious were obliged
to climb an indoor ladder and
look down at the floor to see
how the pieces might fit
together. Only with the
puzzle done could the play
be performed, the one for which
all here, and there, living, and dead,
gathered under the eye of
a legendary director with
a rigorously theoretical,
if deranged, grasp of
dramatic action. Already
half the actors had quit.
But half manage
to hang in, hungry to
commune with a higher
force, and feel some new
aspect of life stir within them.

*

Something somewhere
is eclipsing something else.
Now, suddenly, looking up,
the sky is different. Some
great joy may be about
to transform your life.
The moon glows red.

*

Each day, branches light up,
pink, white, violet, recalling
all that has not blossomed.

Then, even that thought flies.

You're back in an empty house.
Raw burlap on the walls. Nothing
has changed since the 1940s.

The floors seem wet,
almost charred. Would
seem, except it's all so dark.

DEATH IN REVERSE

The Baroness, on her cheek
a postage stamp, foreign, cancelled.

The Baroness, who once stole the crepe from the door
of a funeral home, made a dress of it.

The Baroness, who did not violate the rules,
Bodenheim said, she simply

entered a realm into
which they

couldn't pursue her.

The Baroness, "Death in reverse."

The Baroness, on the streets of New York:

"Death in reverse."

Djuna Barnes thought, upon
seeing the Baroness,
walking toward her

thought the
only thought of
                death that

can be thought,
can be fully thought.

Seeing the
Baroness walking toward one on
the streets of New York,

Djuna Barnes said,
is like seeing

"Death in reverse."

The Baroness, at the beach, poking a dead dog
with a stick, as Barnes observed,
to see what it was made of.

Often with a dog on a leash or several dogs on leashes.
Perhaps with seventy black and purple anklets.

Christmas tree balls as earrings.
A tea strainer around her neck.

A wig of purple and gold.

"Death in reverse."

The Baroness, toward the end,
in the waning days of the Weimar,
selling newspapers on the streets of Berlin.

The Baroness, once a brilliant, joyful sun, one said.
An unparalleled purity said another.

The Baroness, once a sylph
in an entourage of aesthetes.

The Baroness, once in Sorrento,
in a hotel beloved of Nietzsche.

Once by Mt Vesuvius, above the Bay of Naples.
Bedrooms with ceilings like churches,
stairs, hewn rock down to the sea.

The Baroness, once in Venice,
in a pornographic cabinet, inspecting

 the collection of phalluses
"As if they were antique lamps . . ."

"Death in reverse."

The Baroness, once virginal, in a forest
holding a lyre, amid homosexuals in togas.

The Baroness, once an Art Nouveau Orpheus
nodding with narcotic glamour,
as if in the garden of Odilon Redon,
haloed in a field of flowers.

The Baroness, Saturnalian festivals,
her childhood on the Baltic coast:

"We slaughtered pigs. That's what

 pigs are for."

"Death in reverse."

The Baroness, a girl hearing
a beloved tale, "Pious Helena:"

"A fading alcoholic beauty overturns her oil lamp
in a drunken stupor, incinerating herself
then dropping into a boiling cauldron
in hell where her cousin Franz,
a priest and father of her twins,
is waiting for her."

The Baroness, puffing
pot in a China pipe "that must
have held half an ounce or more . . ."

"Death in reverse."

The Baroness, a splayed,
scarlet raincoat: over her nipples,
two tomato cans, held up

with green string around her back.
Between the tomato cans, a very small
bird cage with a live canary.

The Baroness, "amid the turmoil," Ezra Pound said,
"of yids, letts, finns, Estonians, cravats, niberians, Nubians,
Algerians sweeping along 8ᵗʰ Avenue
in the splendor of their vigorous,
unwashed animality."

"Death in reverse."

The Baroness, stripping
bachelors bare, bride with
red nail polish.

"The Baroness is the future," Duchamp said.

The Baroness, "a citizen of terror," Barnes said.

(Perhaps of the ancient city that denied the god,
where was staged the entire drama

of the arrival of Dionysus.

Dionysus, that "death in reverse.")

The Baroness, "looking
at me through blue-white
crazy eyes, saying: 'are you
afraid to let me kiss you?'

 I was shaking all over when I left
the dark stairway, and came out on 14th street . . ."

Arriving at a soiree for an opera singer,
the Baroness: bright blue dress, peacock fan.
On her head, a coal scuttle lid.
Strapped under her chin like a helmet,
two mustard spoons hang
like feathers beside her face.

"Death in reverse."

"I sing only for humanity," the opera singer said.
"I wouldn't lift a leg for humanity," the Baroness said.

The Baroness, smearing
emerald paint on her cheeks.
Eyelashes, gilded porcupine quills.

The Baroness, ropes of dried figs around her neck.

The Baroness, in deep poverty, facing deportation,
speaking to an embassy bureaucrat.
"Rustling coquettishly."
The click of her eyelashes
made her, she says, "irresistible."

"Death in reverse."

The Baroness, expelled from Germany,
denied a visa for France.
Wearing a birthday cake on her head,
not long before her suicide.

"I am," the Baroness said,
"The abode of terror and a snake."

AFTER THE JAPANESE

"My husband is crude
but sufferable, and he
leaves me more or
less alone, on a night of
clear stars, to dream of you."

"My husband is crass
but inattentive, his mind
drifts off into some
abyss, and he falls asleep . . .
I imagine my hands are yours."

"My husband, a drunk,
flits back and forth between
maudlin and morose,
but when he passes out I am
giddy with dreaming of you."

"My husband is mean
but insipid, his cutting
remarks are so lame
I tell them as jokes to my friends,
who know nothing of you."

"My husband is blunt
but routinely evasive,
never talking long;
when he falls silent your
delicate whispers fill my dreams."

"My husband is rich
but improvident. He leaves
his billfold in the
open. So, unwittingly, he
lavishes you with gifts."

"My husband is deaf
to all music, his voice lifted
in song is unbearable;
earbuds in, I am with you,
hearing dream sonatas."

"My husband is gauche
but welcome everywhere.
His very being shames me.
In public, it's pure hell.
Could I not be elsewhere,
in those moments, and
dreaming of you?"

THE LOST COLONY

variations on a poem by John Yau

I

Some cities exist only now
and then, flashing in and out
of the world, depending
how well the song is sung,
or if it's rightly remembered.
Other cities are perpetually
hymned, and shine in the
beyond, like the streets of pearl
Thomas Traherne recollects.
Some great cities are forgotten.
Think of those most ancient
cities of Sumer and Abyssinia,
of which we have only scraps
of the songs their poets sang.
Consider those of modernity,
Saint Petersburg, Istanbul,
Damascus, Cairo, Tulsa,
each still exists only because
their poets sang of them,
lived in them, moved away
from them, suffering exile,
their lives consecrated to
keeping their avowed loci
continually coming into
existence, and continually
passing back into oblivion.

II

Some poets are unhappy,
have no home, while others
are freewheeling roustabouts,
or wanderers, or addicts in
line at a dispensary. Some
are Bedouins who take as
cities dampened campfires:
the smoke, embers, ash, sticks,
any sign of a dispersed gathering,
their loves having left them.
Years back in the hills of China
hermit poets looked down on cities
in the twilight and were glad
to no longer be there, amid
the loneliness and corruption,
those once loved, all gone.
They enjoyed a cup of wine.
Whereas poets of cities like Ys
that disappeared mid-hymn,
the waves pouring in. Their
poets wait to rise again,
as Ys will rise again, once,
or so the prophecy holds,
Paris sinks into the sea.

III

Many cities have streets.
Further, many poets have
walked along those streets,
poets variously dreaming,
lamenting, thinking, observing,
waiting on the ledge of a bank
window in Soho at night for
a new girlfriend, a painter
working as a stripper to
get off work, get a drink.
Often in cities it happens that
poets while walking along
a street will glimpse someone,
or get told how beautiful
someone is, or by chance see
that beautiful person or not
that beautiful person but
another beautiful person,
and fall in love, and that's it.

IV

Cities are where fate happens.
Christmastime. Lights are
up, even in the dive bars,
your new love accepts
an offer to dance, and they
dance, but you're there.
Words get exchanged.
The guy who asked her,
his scalp gets split. Bashed,
it seems, with a beer stein.
Blood abounds. Your new
shirt is ruined. You were
fond of it, but it's soaked,
from the flow of this guy's
head. In that moment you
learn the term for a new
kind of exile, "eighty-sixed."
The bartender says,
"I don't blame you.
The guy had it coming.
But I'm going to have to
eighty-six you, at least
until the New Year."

V

Jerusalem, Paris, Beirut, Granada,
Dublin, Damascus, Florence,
Trieste, Bucharest, Dallas,
poets often write about
their turmoil in exile
from such beloved cities
where their loves still live.

(Poets will often lament
the distance between
where they are, and who
they're with, and where
they'd rather be, and
with whom. Poets
often do not betray the
circumstances of such
distances. In honor of that
reticence, I name no one.)

I will simply say: when
I left New York, the only
TV shows I wanted to watch
were shows shot in New York.
Nothing else mattered.
I was indifferent to the
genre, plot, style, characters,
the suspense, the music. I said
just let me see Manhattan.

Given those years, those
shows were cop shows,
the grittier the better.
Shows like *NYPD Blue*.

I wanted to be the actor
paid to be the corpse
pulled from a dumpster.
The stiff awaiting a
coroner stuck in traffic.

I would be beyond caring
who killed me, or why,
crumpled at the foot
of a root cellar staircase,
or tied to a chair and cut up.
Or in a car in the river.
Or plastic over my once
hopeful, innocent face.
Or dogs find a limb of
mine in a swimming pool.
Or largely intact, I'm bound
on a merry-go-round
looking at the sky with
open eyes in the rain.
I'm dead, ecstatic, and
back in New York!

VI

Blonde, thin, Swedish,
along with Christie Brinkley
Elle McPherson, Yasmin Le Bon,
Bonesy's face was all over New York,
shining forth on magazine
covers, on the sides of
busses, plastered on subways,
on billboards, her gentle, fun-
loving face filled the city
with sexy but ethereal joy
while she was elsewhere,
off on fabulous fashion
shoots, or whirling and
chatting till almost dawn
at high-end dance clubs,
or making a film with
Nastassja Kinski.

Bonesy had a skeletal glamor,
as if she, and all the supermodels
of those early Reagan years,
were all sexy emanations of
a Tibetan death goddess,
otherworldly, immediate,
kindly reminding us, in
shimmering billows of
momentary flesh of the
bitter truth of life's end.
(Her brothers nicknamed
her, still a kid, "Bones.")
Without ever seeing my
cousin, I saw her all the time,

in sweaters and gowns, in
tableaux of exotic pleasure,
on a French beach or by
the fire in an Alpine resort,
always relaxed, happy,
still in essence a tomboy
Catholic schoolgirl.

No camera did not exult in
Bonesy. She was a spirit places
and products summoned unto
themselves so vividly
they filled the mind
of those who saw her
in them and among them.

New to the city I felt guarded,
guided by a girl who once
fell from a tire swing and
broke her arm, who
arriving in New York in
the fullness of her beauty,
ruled over it. Bonesy was
Dakini, bearing blessings.
She was the outward sign of
the island's magical capacities,
whose first boyfriend one
day on a lark sent her
picture to a contest.

Photography lamps.
Their pure glow brightened
even the clear noon daylight.
A ring of bystanders in awe
the one time I saw her,
on Madison. I was walking
back to my office where
I proofread predictions for
a tabloid astrologer.
Bonesy was shooting
an ad as if she had
stepped down into this
dark and unhappy world
from a higher realm of
perfection, of brilliance
beyond all misery,
as if my cousin were
simply light taking,
for the moment of
our lives, the form of
human beauty, there
in the flow of the street.

VII

ghost of O'Hara

A bar where O'Hara
once drank allowed, in the
years following his death,
straight poets to sit and
sip, order more, draw
inspiration, and feel the
residual, fading but
still discernable aura of
Frank, who, some
held, might surprise
everyone and some day
show up, bored with death.

*

Gay men, not always
poets, drank, socialized,
got down and, in honor
of Frank's ghost, did not
contest your presence.
There was just one rule:
never naively dangle
a bandana from either
back pocket. A bandana,
dangling, meant you
were done with being
straight, and were
ready for adventure.

*

A bandana dangling
from your right back
pocket announced: I'm
game for fucking someone
up the ass. From the left,
in the still evolving sign
system of homoerotic
display, a bandana
whispered to the world:
I'm not disinterested
in getting fucked up the ass.

*

There were many, ever
more baroque elaborations
of this queer sign system,
further ways to dangle
a bandana, further ways
to wordlessly sing
your deepest needs
or most fleeting whims:
Fisting, pissing, blow jobs
(given or received), S&M,
or plain old anything goes.
To be straight, to sit, sip,
think of Frank, to be
in that Eden of purest
rapport, was a blessing
from Frank himself.

He saw you from high
up in heaven. He saw
how much you needed
a vision of paradise,
even if it wasn't yours.

VIII

Even in Kyoto, Bashō
said, he still dreamed of
Kyoto. Even not in New York
I dream of New York. Any
given night, I'm there, on
a street, maybe looking up
at a window, as right now
I dream I'm alone in
a wet, shiny alley.

Across the street
a wall's been knocked out.
A few floors up, it's all black inside.
Brightly colored clothes flutter
down, as if a woman's closet
were the site of a bomb blast.
The panoply of colors might be
dresses, scarves, lingerie, long
cherished lavender nightgowns,
blown out by a wind that
rips through her apartment,
perhaps from the Arctic.
Intimate items lie scattered
in a tree, on the sidewalk.
As if some great love
had just now concluded.

Later in any dream I might be
elsewhere in New York, maybe
inside some narrow walk-up,
what should be a railroad flat

but there's always space, massive
interiors where should only be
a modest room. Then a hallway
turns out to be a warehouse,
with a waterfall roaring
down through holes in the
ceiling and disappearing
through holes in the floor,
silvery cascades thundering
down from above while
a white mist is rising up
from the plunge into
some cavernous pit
as the ghost of Coleridge,
there with me, notes:
The continuous
change of the Matter, the
perpetual sameness of the Form . . .

IX

where affection holds no steady mansion

The scam reached right into
the heart of their newly formed
household, these two lovers
who would almost marry,
but then, catastrophically,
not. The scam had little
bearing on what their love
would prove to be.

At first, she was exhilarated in her
retelling, believing, hoping,
fate would free her,
praying the scam would
prove not to be a scam,
and that she had helped
those with no place to turn.
But as the strangeness of
her adventure over the last
few hours out of the house
became perceptible to her,
she grew frightened.

Gripping a knotted handkerchief
which she, then, threw down
on the bed, believing it to be
a gnarl of dollars, an assured
but unexamined return for
her courage on behalf of
a hapless couple met
at the cash machine,

foreign, abject, needing
help from someone kind
who knew this country and
its weird, inhospitable ways.

She was hyper, more so
than usual. And she looked
 – because of her increasingly
evident vulnerability, – more
beautiful and tragic than ever,
idealistic, trusting, shaking,
dark-haired, confiding a mile
a minute while realizing,
in the complex drama of
the tale of her afternoon, she'd
handed over money, a lot,
gone with them, somewhere,
withdrawn even more money.
They took her money away,
said they brought it back, having,
with the indispensable help
of her cash, secured a long
awaited inheritance they could not,
it turned out, take with them
to their home country.

If it would not be a further
imposition on her generous
nature, an abuse of her time spent
in the service of the unfortunate,
she, could she, distribute
the extra money included in
the return of her cash, to churches

and charities? They put, they said,
a wryly charming spell on
the kerchief-wrapped bundle,
a spell popular and effective
where they came from,
a spell to make her, they said,
lucky in love. But she had to
promise not to untie the
handkerchief till she was
back in that safest of places,
her new apartment, with
her new love. They should,
a native folk belief had it,
only open it together.

The thieves blessed her.
She, in turn, thanked them,
thanked them for having, out of
their own unasked-for difficulties,
brought a blessing upon her
new household, her new love.
She was excited, proud of
herself, for not giving in
to prejudice, to fear, to basic
urban indifference, proud
she embodied, for a few
hours, all that was best
about the city she loved,
proud she had, out of
the blue, participated in
a meaningful charitable act,
proud that she had the clarity
required for a virtuous action,
so rare in modern life. She

was actually helping. She
had performed a mitzvah,
one both her orthodox and
her communist ancestors
in their respective afterlives
would deem laudable, would
judge to be truly ethical.

The power of spell they
cast on her was dwindling
in that new hallway, was
vanishing in that new
apartment where the
couple lived in love,
having just moved in
together, having had,
already, difficulties but
also great happiness.
It was natural, wasn't it,
the time drawing close,
to think about marriage?

She was shaking, not
yet sobbing, joy being
swallowed up in shame
and dread. She was smart,
accomplished, a caring
young woman, not at all
new to the city, yet, on a
sunny Saturday, she'd
been taken in, been
expertly manipulated,
been flat out robbed.

Then she was crying, sobbing,

asking, would he unknot
the kerchief, pour out
on the bed if not the
promised dollars the
horrible rolls of dollar-sized
scraps of newspapers and
advertising inserts for
electronics and getaway
Caribbean vacations.
Her noble gesture now
felt dead to all virtue.

Profiled, picked out, fooled,
had lavish emotions stirred,
been entranced by a fantastic
tale with a base end, she felt,
in that moment, much that
she prized about herself,
about what it meant to be
moral, had been mercilessly
destroyed. Unveiled, the scam
just kept going on, deep inside
her, going on from then on,
in both their hearts. This
idyllic new apartment,
this joyful hope of a life
together, had they both been
marked? Been told a tale?
Been ennobled, charmed,
drawn ever more deeply
in, only to be swindled by
Eros himself, the god who
planned all of this, this first,
and least cruel, of the coming

consequences of their still
gathering, still unfolding
love for each other?

X

9/11

True, I was not there,
had already begun
my exile from the city,
from, that is, the heart
of all poetry. I did
not see the smoke,
the poisonous dust,
rolling up the streets,
or pick from the air
sheets of embossed
stationery floating
down from an office
that instantly no
longer existed.

XI

In sleep I kept going back,
seeing caverns, hollows, holes,
secret places, closets that
were the inside of a cathedral,
train stations where the dome
was the Arctic night sky,
the aurora borealis pulsing
green and purple above
Grand Central Station.
Last night a child was lost
there, a little girl. As a favor
to her mother I was minding
her but she wandered off.
I panicked. I raced around.
(Were you simply my soul
could I have lost you
any more quickly?)
I gave up. Got coffee.
I worried what I would
tell her mother, whatever
goddess that was, who
had asked just this one
simple favor of me.
Then, out of the blue,
the girl walks up to me,
joined me at the table,
and we shared some
sweet Zabar's treat.

XII

Painters the world was yet to hear of
were also sleeping nearby. Also
sleeping nearby were painters
the world will never hear of.
They, too, plucked colors and
images from the depths of
their heads. Though beyond
fulfilling the demands of their art
they too, all the painters, known,
not yet known, never to be known,
as Borges did Buenos Aires, were
dreaming Soho into existence.
I was so new to the city those
nights I never knew what part
we were wandering in. Years
later, turning a corner, or rising
up to the street from the train,
I knew I'd been there, late on
a dark night, knocking around
with other young painters and
poets led on from one after
hours bar to the next by the
one we called Sergeant Dave.

Had he been in Nam? None
knew. Nonetheless, when
heading out to recon the
aesthetic war zone of lower
Manhattan, summer nights,
quiet, vacant, deserted blocks

lit as much by starlight as
streetlights, we called him that:

Sergeant Dave.

At this extreme distance from
those nights all that is known of
the identity of Sergeant Dave
is that he liked to drink, drive,
drink more, drive more, and
always and only after midnight.
Sergeant Dave had a van. He
took us all around the lower
edge of the island. He'd learned
a lot about modern art in the army,
especially about the glories of
abstraction. But Sergeant Dave
didn't want to be a painter
or a poet anymore. He just liked
to park the van then walk the
empty underworld of Soho
amazed how quiet New York City
could be where no one was at night.

Everyone I met on those nights
knocking around with Sergeant Dave
came from nowhere, to find out
about art, to see, and fall in love,
and fail in love, and fail at art,
and then make the art that
arose from such agonies of love
as could only ever be felt amid

the ongoing cosmic wars of light
and dark to which, as if unawares,
Sergeant Dave had born witness.

His close friend, my recent
acquaintance, John Yau, had
just written a poem inexplicable
and strangely beautiful, more so
than any I'd read. It was a wave of
hallucinatory fragments in a
disorienting, mesmerizing flow
which I only now associate
with my life, then and now,
with being initiated by these
midnight tours of sacred duty,
with Sergeant Dave, who, it would
seem, had his own affinity for
empty and infinite spaces.

Who was Boullée? Why did his
life have such scenes as appeared in
"Scenes from the Life of Boullée?"
Scenes that seemed taken from
the life none of us had yet lived,
unless we were, in some yet to
be clarified way, to be visionary
Enlightenment era French architects
designing unbuildable cenotaphs
based on the innate symbolic
qualities of the cube, pyramid,
cylinder and sphere, the interior
a hollow globe, the universe.

Those nights of serious drinking
were we each at home in bed,
dreaming and dead, Soho our
cenotaph, perhaps learning
about alchemy from the ghost
of Sir Isaac Newton? Did none
of us exist? Did John Yau, drifting
off to sleep, in a derelict walk-up
on Crosby Street strung with
extension cords hooked up to
clip-on lights and space heaters,
himself always imagining
nonexistent visionary spaces,
himself an architect of shadows,
his words formed out of deep
recesses cut in a stone that
reflected no light yet giving
the reader the sense they were
as if by magic floating in the air,
borne in the wake of images
in the immensity of space?

Breeze from the river. Light
in the wrinkles of the flowing.
A diner was there. After a night
of wandering and drinking,
we'd have a delicious breakfast.
The sky would lighten. Then
Sergeant Dave, dropping each
of us off in his van, drove back
to his place in Hoboken.

XIII

lament

This time, she's a redhead,
attractive all over again
while you, in your
serviceable, not quite
ideal reincarnation,
look like a long-forgotten
character actor, of
no particular
distinction, in films
negligently preserved,
concerning which not
even fanatical
film scholars much
regret the loss of.
Inside your head
a ghost slides close:
"Once again, this
won't work out.")

XIV

That farewell to an ex
glimpsed by chance on
the lower part of the island,
Soho empty, years ago,
"The Lost Colony," that
hymn to hopelessness,
having just been written.
(Tribeca, did it exist?)

Back then, whatever you
wrote back left me awe-
struck and uncomprehending,
even when the poem
hinted how to read it.
Like Giotto, you showed
only the back of the
head in a painting to
to say the drama is
going on elsewhere.

From the start your
words shone with heart,
imagination, invention,
dazzle, misdirection, blunt
artful confessions, and
not a little hilarity.

To distract, perhaps
from understanding we
were lost residents of yet
another doomed outpost.

Roanoke, the lost colony
haunting every American
child, perhaps doubly
those children who
hail from China, so that
all places are just lost
colonies, full of hopeful
people soon to be
struck from all
historical record.

Was the Lost Colony
a post-mortal land of
non-being, as much
as an historical fact?

John, I think you saw
a vanishing Manhattan.
I think you saw we'd all
just be there a short while.
I think you saw we'd
all be gone, leaving
no word cut in a tree,
not even love's initials,
not even in the further-
most place from Earth,
maybe the lote tree,
edge of the seventh
heaven, through which
each soul passes in the
annihilation of love.

XV

And the woman, seen then,
stepping down into the dark
of the subway stair, that Aurelia,
that Nadja, that dancer in
Bruges-la-Mort, that Unica
Zürn, that Eternal Beloved,
was once again gone, was,
at that moment, disappearing,
for you, right there, already,
that afternoon, no more
than a name, or was it
Mott, Mercer, Sullivan?
Wherever it was, it was a
street in a Symbolist novel.
A street in a Symbolist novel
where the double of a past
love keeps turning down
an even darker street, turning
away forever, vanishing
among the many alluring,
enigmatic art world women
in your poems who, when
they fixed a scarf, or make
a knowing remark about
the glory of form, become
the ultimate other, become
the erotic embodiment of
the possibilities of the city,
of all cities, Paris, Bruges,
Berlin, London, New York,
or at least, of the essence
of New York, Soho, become
the beauty you moved here

to meet, so many moved
here to meet, a spirit, sadly
only sensed in vanishing,
glimpsed on a street,
vanishing as could only
ever happen in the narrow
end of your island, our island,
where rivers flow out
and ocean begins.

XVI

Were we sensing
much to be
hopeless,
but sublimely so,
even as Soho,
this other
Roanoke,
this other
abandonment,
this further hint of
every disappearance,
those already
felt and others
yet to come.
Where does
everyone
keep going,
year after year
lifetime after
lifetime?
To some more
perfect and
ethereal
Manhattan,
where once luckless
lovers find each
other,
nameless
and ecstatic,
while becoming
a cool, discrete,
invisible

flame within
the living
memory of
those still here,
still dreaming farewell?

GHOST OF KAWABATA

A bride's mind, as it does,

      wanders.

   *

Refined desires

      find ways to shine.

   *

Then said an art ingénue, from France,
before the altar

of an artwork: "Much about
    the symbolists

is abhorrent,

      but not all."

   *

She loves, she goes on to confess,

The Abyss.

Two women. One
naked,

       facing some

twilit depth,

holds a smoking heart.

    *

Another, clothed, indolent,

sleeps under a tree.

Over her   a fluttering demon.

      (Her thighs plunge
      upward, and

      disappear
      into shadows.)

    *

Later, outside, in
the cresting solitude,

a crow closes its wings
and daylight

folds
into darkness.

      *

The sun the simple knot
that holds up the

sundress of day.

      *

      (Her allure a mix of
      impulsive speech

      and cold
      thoughts.)

      *

After the war, Kawabata
      revealed to his translator

a bohemian ruin obliterated by

the firebombing,

a lost paradise of
geishas and deviants,

of a fully lived
aestheticism.

*

Blackening, brightening,

the wrinkled sheet of

the Hudson, the
river that

brought you

great love, then

took it away.

*

The sky shines in the water.
The green of your shirt

matches your eyes, she said,
which you had previously

believed to be blue.

*

She liked, back then,
in the early days

of your delirium, to let her
kimono fall open,

the sash too
casually tied.

*

Certain murders
excited her. Talk of

them quickly
led to bed.

GHOST OF KAWABATA II

Young lovers
rapt, in the park, you

keep forgetting their anguish.

*

Ripples of black ink
and silver, the sun falling,

shadows cover the river,
salt smell under

the pier.

*

A long-ago love, now dissolute,

spends her evenings

at meetings.

A long-ago love,

once so measured in
her ecstasies, now just a drunk.

*

Salt scent, tide
infiltrating the river.

Your mouth wet with
remembering

the lubricant, the
smeared, shining gel.

*

She, back from the bathroom,

diaphragm, nestled

in a delicious

place.

*

A long-ago love,
still quite beautiful,

even, now, in the
present of only memory,

turning away.

446

*

Tradition unconceals a truth:
every part of your house

is now on fire.
Tradition tells you,

lie down and sob.

*

A different tradition tells you
your love had a rose

stitched

in glitter
across the front of

her sweater.

*

An infection inflames

the rim of your eye.

*

Among the ghosts

with you in limbo are:
Gide, Cavafy, and Kawabata.

*

Kawabata
    whispering

            "Ugliness is
often   more memorable . . ."

PASSING CLARITIES

for Nathaniel Tarn and Janet Rodney

Lava washed clean of
any trace of burning,
scent of dry wood
and bluish grey pines,
this ecotone of mountains
and unremitting heat,
a suffering Christ
on a black cross.

*

Centurions' spearpoint
much multiplied, more
like a bullet-ridden
massacre victim hoisted
up over the world.
Wounds on thighs.
The horsehair hair
lifts in chapel currents.
Glass eyes shimmering
in imitation of tears.

*

Nosebleed wind.
Menstrual arroyos.
Buñuel's San Simeon

hallucinating on a pillar,
Catherine Deneuve
pouring licentiousness
on her hot breath
into a chaste ear.
Blood streaming down
the clay-colored arm
into the armpit of the Christ.

*

Hollowing wind heard
through brush above
scampering claws.
Mineral glint. Desert.
Pure glowing earth,
flat, vacant miles,
canyons. The wind
takes earth away.
Though this is not
1944. Not divine light,
the top blown off
the kiva of the world.

*

Lead me, spider god,
higher into hills the
color of a flowerpot
or a scuffed eraser
schoolyear's end.

*

Coils in stone, of stone,
amber, ocher
in layered slices,
hot pink in late sun.
Goats in a grove. Toe
holds in stone.
Blue-green shade.
Limestone.

A TREE ON FIRE

after Charles Birchfield

Black trunk, glowing gold.

                    Leaves of fire,

fire disinclined
to burn, reluctant, in fact,

to light up the ragged sketch of
olive and cinnamon.

As if an afterthought of the light,
were coming through,

behind the grey-
black trunk.

A tree in a field. A road.
Two dirt ruts running
to the outline
of a village.

In a field: fall and spring at once.

Long grasses bend towards the horizon.

(A wind must be coming up.)

Bands of pale green
top faded tufts.

Autumn ignites the tree.

Autumn calls to spring
        through the medium of

        purple and yellow flowers.

In the foreground leaves
looking like arrows direct

attention past the tree to
somewhere hidden.

Why else would wind
turn all thought toward what
the world can offer
no glimpse of?

                *

Overhead, a moody conflagration,
a fire not yet the crown of
the tree before you,

whose branches darken
as the brightness keeps building,
branches seeming to hold back
a light too diffuse to be

sunlight, too close to
the aura of the branches

not to be their agony,

the outward sign of
ecstatic distress.

*

A large tree must be behind me.

Or next to where I am,
in October, in sunlight,
in some countryside,
where the tree that
can be seen

confesses frankly to
the hell of reuniting
heaven and earth.

*

Waves of energy
radiate from the tree, touches of
red in the trembling.

*

In one spot, the last of
some long suffering not
yet given over to bliss.

*

Upswept limbs, human arms
lifted, as if celebrating
that in winter, all will be
barren. But this is not then,
is not yet then. This burning
brings winter to be
in an ecstasy.

*

In such a field, along
such a road, shouldn't there be

a small county hospital

where the stricken see
this tree, can recall, then,

what a miracle the
body is, even the

pained, afflicted,
savaged body?

*

A surge of wind across a field
is told by the tree it passes through:

Let the dying be mindful,
one last time, of what

dying is a part of.
But you, my soul, are
you even here? How
can you not be? I feel your
fury, your gold glow, apart from
and around me, as within
myself I raise my arms
to the sky in praise of
your visit, that you
might find me, here,
find me, and cast a glow
around all living things,
in the field, in the village,
in what is behind or
beside or above me.
Stripped, dry, shaken
by that life flooding
freely into a secret field,
I feel torn open (though
from a distance
I appear to be in
the center of light,
to be, at core, to be of
an inextinguishable gold.)

ABOUT THE AUTHOR

JOSEPH DONAHUE's most recent volumes of poetry are *Musica Callada* and *Near Star* (Verge Books, 2024), volumes four and five of his ongoing poem cycle, *Terra Lucida*. Other recent works are *Wind Maps I-VII* (Talisman 2018), *The Disappearance of Fate* (Spuyten Duyvil, 2019), and *Infinite Criteria* (Black Square Editions 2022). He is the co-translator of *First Mountain*, by Zhang Er. With Edward Foster he edited *The World in Time and Space: Towards a History of Innovative American Poetry, 1970-2000* (Talisman, 2002). He teaches in the English Department at Duke University.

Author Photo by Star Black